FOUR GOSPELS. ONE STORY.

SAVIOR

FOUR GOSPELS. ONE STORY.

SAVIOR

A fresh look at Jesus Christ, His Ministry, and His teachings

JACK J. BLANCO

Autumn House® Publishing
www.autumnhousepublishing.com
A Division of **REVIEW AND HERALD® PUBLISHING**
Since 1861

Published by Autumn House® Publishing, a division of Review and Herald˚ Publishing, Hagerstown, MD 21741-1119

Autumn House® titles may be purchased in bulk for educational, business, fund-raising, or sales promotional use. For information, please e-mail SpecialMarkets@reviewandherald.com.

Autumn House® Publishing publishes biblically based materials for spiritual, physical, and mental growth and Christian discipleship.

The author assumes full responsibility for the accuracy of all facts and quotations as cited in this book.

This book was
Edited by Gerald Wheeler
Copyedited by James Cavil
Designed by Trent Truman
Cover illustration: *The Lamb of God,* by Nathan Greene © 2000. All rights reserved.
           To learn more about the artist, please visit www.hartclassics.com;
           background image: © idizimage/stockphoto.com
Interior designed by Heather Rogers
Typeset: Bembo 11/13

PRINTED IN U.S.A.

12 11 10 09 08   5 4 3 2 1

Library of Congress Cataloging-in-Publication Data
Blanco, Jack J., 1929-   .
  Savior: four Gospels, one story: a conversational paraphrase / Jack J. Blanco.
    p. cm.
1. Bible. N.T. Gospels—Harmonies, English. 2. Jesus Christ—Biography—Sources, Biblical. I. Title.
BT299.3B53 2008
226'.1—dc22
                    2008005143

ISBN 978-0-8127-0469-3

Preface

Savior is a paraphrase of the four Gospels (Matthew, Mark, Luke, and John) woven into one narrative. I have written it from the perspective of trying to communicate to young people in my classes the thoughts—not so much the theology—of the gospel for them to understand and put into practice more fervently what Jesus lived and taught.

Through the years a number of scholars have attempted to harmonize the four Gospels by placing them in parallel columns, such as A. T. Robertson's *A Harmony of the Gospels for Students of the Life of Christ* (Harper and Brothers, 1922); Ralph D. Heim's *A Harmony of the Gospels for Students* (Minneapolis: Fortress Press, 1947); and Orville E. Daniel's *An Interwoven Harmony of the Gospels* (Welch Publishing Company, 1986). Some commentaries have attempted to harmonize the Gospels by simply referencing the texts.

While the overall flow of the four Gospel accounts from the birth of Jesus to His crucifixion and resurrection is quite consistent, we do find differences of perspectives in the individual Gospels. For instance, Matthew narrates the story of Jesus from a Jewish perspective and Luke from that of a Gentile. Tradition understands that Mark recorded what he heard from Peter, and John, who with Matthew was an eyewitness, writes about Jesus as the beloved incarnate Son of God.

Examining the Gospels more closely reveals a difference in the sequence of the temptations of Christ in the wilderness listed in Matthew 4:1-11 and Luke 4:1-13. Numeric variations also appear in the experience of Jesus with the Gadarenes. Did one demon-possessed man challenge Him, as in Mark 5:1-20 and Luke 8:26-39, or two men, as in Matthew 8:28-34? And while all of the Gospels relate the feeding of the 5,000, only Matthew and Mark tell about the 4,000.

Then we puzzle over the problem of duplication of stories. Matthew 8:19-22 and Luke 9:57-62 relate the story about a young man's desire to follow Jesus, but his father had just died. While the stories are the same, the context is different. In Matthew the incident takes place amid various healings, while in Luke it appears in the midst of the rejection of Jesus in

Samaria. Matthew 23:37, Luke 13:34, and Luke 19:41 make it seem that Jesus wept over Jerusalem several different times.

The setting of certain parables may differ. In Luke 19:11-27 Jesus gives the parable of the talents *prior* to His triumphal entry into Jerusalem (Luke 19:28-40), while in Matthew 25:14-30 essentially the same parable *follows* the triumphal entry (Matt. 21:1-11).

Luke may have recorded the accounts of eyewitnesses in the sequence as he heard them, not being too concerned where to place individual stories, as long as the larger picture from Jesus' birth to Calvary and His resurrection remained consistent. It is also possible that individual events occurred more than once. In spite of such minor differences, we observe an underlying harmony throughout the four Gospels.

The compiler is left to decide how to handle these slight differences if he or she wishes to harmonize the Gospels into one unified story. It is for this purpose that I have decided to combine the four narratives.

I wish to thank Jolena King and Star Stevens for proofreading the manuscript and giving so unselfishly of their time to make this book more reader-friendly.

—Jack J. Blanco

Contents

one

Birth and Childhood of Jesus

My dear friend, let me tell you what has happened these past few years. There are many oral and some written reports about Jesus from those who both saw and heard Him and know what He did. With God's Spirit guiding me, I want to summarize for you what I've heard from reliable witnesses and read in the written accounts that I carefully examined. Then you can know for sure what Christians believe. This is the story of Jesus, the Messiah, God's beloved Son (Luke 1:1-4; Mark 1:1).

From the beginning God's Son was there. There never was a time when He did not exist. He is also the Word of God. All things were made by Him, and nothing came into being without Him. He is the source of life, and His life on earth was like a bright light in the darkness that brought hope to everyone. He came to His own people, but most of them did not accept Him. Those who did were born again and became sons and daughters of God. It was not because they willed it or because they were Jews—it was by the power of God. So the Word of God became a human being and lived among us. He came to us from God full of grace and truth (John 1:1-5, 10-14).

At the appropriate time God sent a man named John to tell people about that Light. He was not the Light, but was to point to it. That Light was Jesus, the Son of the living God. John spoke boldly of Him, saying, "This is the One I've been telling you about. He is much more important than I am. You must listen to Him. Even though He is younger than I am, He existed before I was born."

It is through Jesus that we've been blessed. Moses gave people the law, which was all he could do, but Jesus gave us grace and truth. No one has seen God face to face except the Son of God, who came directly from the Father to show us what God is like (John 1:6-9, 15-18).

Surprise Announcement

During the days of Herod the Great a priest named Zechariah and his wife, Elizabeth, lived in Judea. They were both descendants of Aaron, the brother of Moses, and were good people living by God's commandments. But they had no children and were too old to have any.

One day as Zechariah was ministering at the Temple in Jerusalem he went into the holy place to offer incense. A lot of people were outside praying. Suddenly an angel appeared, standing on the right side of the altar of incense. Zechariah was terrified. The angel said, "Don't be afraid, Zechariah. God has heard your prayers. Your wife, Elizabeth, will give birth to a son, and you are to name him John. Both you and your wife will be very happy because of him, and many people will rejoice with you. He will do a great work for the Lord. He must never drink wine or any kind of alcohol. He will be filled with the Holy Spirit from the day of his birth, and during his ministry he will bring many people to the Lord. He will preach with the spirit and power of Elijah, softening the hearts of parents toward their children and children toward their parents. He will prepare the way for the Messiah. Many will turn their lives around and become good people, honest and just in all they do."

Zechariah asked, "How can this be? I'm an old man, and my wife is also up in years."

The angel replied, "I am Gabriel. I stand in the presence of God. He is the one who sent me to bring you the good news. Because you doubt the truth of what I have said, let me give you a sign to help you believe. You will lose your ability to speak for nine months, until the baby is born."

Meanwhile, the people outside were wondering why it was taking Zechariah so long to offer incense. When he finally came out, he couldn't talk, and the people concluded from his gesturing that he must have had a vision or seen an angel. Zechariah completed his week of service at the Temple and then returned home.

Soon afterward, Elizabeth became pregnant. She praised the Lord and said, "God is good! He has answered my prayer and given me a baby in my old age!" For the next five months she remained in seclusion, until it was evident that the Lord had removed her disgrace of not having had children (Luke 1:5-25).

Gabriel Visits Mary

Six months after Elizabeth became pregnant, God sent the angel Gabriel to the little village of Nazareth in the province of Galilee to a young woman named Mary. She was engaged to be married to a carpenter named Joseph, whose ancestor was King David. Gabriel said,

"Greetings, Mary! Of all the women in Israel, you are the most blessed." Mary was terrified and confused about what the angel was saying. The angel spoke gently: "Don't be afraid. God has chosen to bless you. You will become pregnant and will give birth to a son. God wants you to name Him Jesus. He will be the Son of God and will do great things for the Most High. God will give Him the throne of His ancestor David. He will rule over Israel, and His kingdom will never end."

Mary asked, "How can this be? I am not even married yet and am still a virgin."

The angel answered, "The Holy Spirit's power will make it happen, and the Baby born to you will be holy. He will be the Messiah, the Son of the living God. Your cousin Elizabeth is pregnant in her old age. She's already six months along and will also give birth to a son. With God nothing is impossible."

Mary responded, "I'm the Lord's servant. May it happen to me as you have said." Then the angel disappeared (Luke 1:26-38).

Mary Visits Elizabeth

A few days after the angel Gabriel visited Mary, she left Galilee for Judea to visit her cousin Elizabeth. When she got there, she told Elizabeth about the angel Gabriel's visit and everything he had said. As Elizabeth listened to Mary, the baby inside of her responded with joy. And the Holy Spirit inspired Elizabeth to say, "Mary, God has blessed you above all the women in Israel, and He will bless that precious baby you're carrying. What an honor that the mother of Israel's Messiah should come and visit me! As I was listening to you, the baby inside of me jumped for joy! Bless your heart, you believed what the angel said, and now you too are pregnant! That means that all the other things the angel told you will also happen."

Mary, inspired by the Holy Spirit, responded, "I too want to praise the Lord! I love Him with all my heart. He is my God and Savior. He took notice of me, His lowly servant, and now people will know me as the woman who gave birth to the Messiah. The Mighty One has made this happen. Bless His name forever.

"In every generation God has been kind to those who honor Him. His mighty arm scattered those who were proud. He removed kings from their thrones and exalted the lowly. He fed the hungry and satisfied them with good things, while the rich went away empty. He has always helped Israel and has not forsaken His people. He has not forgotten the promise He made to Abraham that He would be merciful to him and his children forever."

Then Elizabeth insisted that Mary stay with her for the next three months until Elizabeth's baby was born. So Mary did, and then she went back home (Luke 1:39-56).

Birth of John

Elizabeth had her baby as expected, and it was a boy. Word quickly spread to relatives and friends that all had gone well. They knew that the Lord had been with her for her to deliver a baby so easily at her age, and they all rejoiced.

When the baby was 8 days old, he was circumcised, and all the relatives, friends, and neighbors who could came for the naming ceremony. They suggested that Elizabeth name the baby Zechariah, after his father.

But Elizabeth said, "No. We're naming him John."

The relatives said, "What? There's no one in our family history named John."

So they asked the father. He motioned for something to write on, and to everyone's surprise he wrote, "The boy's name will be John."

Suddenly Zechariah could speak again, just as the angel had said he would, and the first thing Zechariah did was to praise God.

Relatives and neighbors were surprised to hear the old man talk again. News of what had happened spread throughout the Judean hills. Everyone who heard it took it to heart and asked themselves, "What kind of man will this baby grow up to be?" From that moment on, the Lord was with little John in a special way.

While Zechariah was still praising the Lord, the Holy Spirit came upon him, and he made this prophecy: "Praise the Lord! He has come to redeem His people. He has shown us His power by sending us a Savior from the lineage of David. As He said through His prophets long ago, 'I will save you from your enemies and from all those who hate you.' God is merciful and will not forget the promise He made to our father Abraham. He will keep His word and deliver us from our enemies so that we can serve Him without fear and live righteously all of our days.

"And you, my little son, will grow up to be the Lord's prophet and will prepare the way for Him to come. You will help people accept the Savior so that they will be forgiven for their sins. You will help them know God's tender love and mercy. Then His grace will break upon us. It will shine on those in spiritual darkness who are living in the shadow of eternal death and will guide all of us in the way of peace."

As John grew, he became physically and spiritually stronger every day. When he was grown, he made his home in the wilderness until he began his public ministry in the hills of Judea (Luke 1:57-80).

Birth of Jesus

Here are some details about how Jesus was born. While His mother Mary was still engaged to be married to Joseph, who was a carpenter from Nazareth, she became pregnant by the power of the Holy Spirit. Joseph decided to break the engagement quietly and to give up plans for the wedding. Then Mary could have her baby somewhere else to minimize her embarrassment.

But one night an angel appeared to Joseph in a dream and said, "Joseph, don't be disappointed in Mary. She is still a virgin. Go ahead and marry her. Don't worry about what the relatives and neighbors think. The baby she carries is from the power of the Holy Spirit. She will have a Son, and you are to name Him Jesus, because He will save His people from their sins."

All this was predicted centuries ago by the Jewish prophet Isaiah when he said, "A virgin will conceive and have a Son, and He will be called Emmanuel, which means 'God has become one of us.'"

So Joseph went ahead and married Mary, as the angel had advised. But he had no sexual relations with her until after the Son of God was born. And he named the baby Jesus, just as the angel had said (Matt. 1:18-25).

About the time Jesus was to be born, Caesar Augustus ordered a tax registration to be taken throughout the Roman Empire. As you know, this took place when Quirinius was governor of Syria and the surrounding territories. Everyone was required to register in the city of their ancestors. So Joseph, who lived in Nazareth in the province of Galilee, had to go to Bethlehem in Judea to register, because he was a descendant of David. He had to take his wife, Mary, with him, who was about to have her baby. Because all the rooms in town were full, an innkeeper let them stay overnight in his barn. It was there that she gave birth to her firstborn son, wrapped Him in strips of cloth, and laid Him in one of the animal's feeding boxes.

It was the time of year that shepherds stayed with their flocks all night in the field. Suddenly one night an angel of the Lord appeared, flooding the fields with glory. The shepherds were scared.

The angel said to them, "Don't be afraid. I bring you good news for people everywhere. Today the Savior of the world was born in Bethlehem. This is how you will recognize Him: Look for Him in a barn, wrapped in strips of cloth, and lying in an animal's feeding box."

Then the whole sky lit up, and a host of angels sang, "Glory to God in the highest, and peace and goodwill on earth to those who love Him."

As soon as the angels left, the shepherds said to one another, "Come, let's go to Bethlehem and find this baby the angels were talking about."

So they took off for Bethlehem. There they found Mary and Joseph in a barn and the baby wrapped in strips of cloth, lying in an animal's feeding box. They told them everything that had happened out in the fields. When people heard what the shepherds said about this baby, many were amazed and gave serious thought to what the shepherds told them. But Mary treasured their testimony in her heart and often considered what it might all mean.

Then the shepherds went back out to the fields to take care of their sheep, praising God for what they had seen and heard in the barn and from the angel (Luke 2:1-20).

Jesus Is Dedicated

When the Baby was 8 days old, He was circumcised and named Jesus, just as the angel had told Joseph before the baby was born. Forty days later the parents brought Him to the Temple to be dedicated to the Lord according to the stipulation of Moses: "Every firstborn son must be set aside for the Lord to acknowledge God's special claim on him." As an offering, Joseph brought two pigeons, because he and Mary were too poor to buy a lamb.

An old man named Simeon lived in Jerusalem. He was a good man and very devout, always in the Temple praying for the Messiah to come and save Israel. The Holy Spirit had told him that he would not die before he saw the Messiah. The morning that Mary and Joseph came to the Temple to dedicate their son, the Holy Spirit told Simeon to go there early to meet them. When he saw the baby, he knew this was the Messiah. He took little Jesus from Mary's arms, held Him up, and praised God, saying, "O Lord, You have kept Your promise to me. You have let me live to see the Messiah! He is the Light of the world and the glory of Your people Israel!"

Joseph and Mary were amazed at all the things that Simeon said about little Jesus. Then he handed the baby back to Mary, blessed her, and said, "This Child will be rejected by many in Israel, but many others will accept Him with joy. This will show whether people love God or not. And when you hear what some will say, it will be like a knife going into your heart."

There also was a prophet named Anna in the Temple that morning. She was from the tribe of Asher. Her husband had died after they had been married for only seven years, and she was now 84 years old. She could be found in the Temple almost any time day or night, fasting, praying, and worshipping God.

When Simeon finished talking to Mary and Joseph, Anna came up and began praising God. Then she turned and talked to everyone who would listen about the baby who had come to be king and deliver Israel.

After Joseph and Mary fulfilled the requirements for dedicating the baby, they found a room in Bethlehem before returning to Nazareth. There the boy Jesus grew up, healthy and strong, blessed by God and filled with wisdom beyond his years (Luke 2:21-40; Matt. 2:8-12).

Wise Men Come to Visit

Before Joseph and Mary left Bethlehem to return to Nazareth, some Wise Men from a country east of Palestine came to Jerusalem, asking the people, "Where can we find the newborn King of Israel? For weeks we've been following a very bright star that led us to Jerusalem. We believe this unusual star is a sign of the birth of the Deliverer King. We want to be among the first to worship Him."

This happened when Herod the Great was king. When he heard about the Wise Men and what they were saying, he was deeply disturbed and saw this as a plot to overthrow his government. So he called for the leading priests and teachers and demanded, "Who is this baby King? Where did the prophets say He was to be born?"

They told him they didn't know anything about a baby King, but according to Scripture the Messiah would be born in Bethlehem. They quoted Micah's prophecy: "O Bethlehem in Judah, you are not just another small town. But you will be the birthplace of the promised King of Israel."

Herod dismissed the priests and teachers and sent a message to the Wise Men to see him. When they came, he welcomed them and asked them about their trip and questioned when they had first seen this unusual star. They visited for a while, and then Herod suggested that they go on to Bethlehem to find the baby King, and come back and tell him so that he could go and worship him too.

As the Wise Men left the palace, they saw the star again. It guided them to Bethlehem and stopped over the house where Joseph and Mary were now staying. Joseph welcomed them, and when they saw the baby, the Wise Men fell on their knees and worshipped Him. Then they gave the family gifts of gold, costly incense, and perfume. That night God warned the men in a dream not to go back to Herod, for he would harm the Child. So they went home another way (Matt. 2:1-12).

Safety in Egypt

God also spoke to Joseph in a dream and said, "Get up, take Mary and the baby and leave for Egypt immediately, because in the morning Herod will send palace guards to find the Baby and kill Him. You must stay in Egypt until I tell you to come back."

Joseph woke up Mary and told her what God had said. Mary agreed they should go quickly. Soon they were ready. He helped her and the baby on to the donkey, and in the middle of the night they left for Egypt. They stayed there until Herod died. This was what the prophet Hosea had predicted years before when he spoke for God, saying, "I will call my Son from Egypt."

When Herod heard that the Wise Men had left the area and gone home another way, he was furious! So he sent palace guards to kill all the babies in and around Bethlehem who were 2 years old and under. The prophet Jeremiah had predicted this when he said: "There will come a time that the anguished cry of mothers will be heard in southern Judah over the slaughter of their babies. They will refuse to be comforted."

Some time after the slaughter of the babies, Herod died. Then an angel of the Lord appeared to Joseph again in a dream and said, "You may now take Mary and the Child back home, because the king is dead." Joseph obeyed and immediately left for home with Mary and the Child. But when he crossed the border and heard that Herod's cruel son Archelaus had taken his father's place, he was afraid. Then God spoke to Joseph in another dream and told him not to settle in Jerusalem but to go back to Nazareth. This too was according to several prophets who predicted that the Messiah would be called a Nazarene (Matt. 2:13-23).

The Boy Jesus

Once every year Joseph and Mary would go to Jerusalem for the Passover. When Jesus was 12 years old, they took Him along. After the Passover, crowds of people left the city, but Jesus lingered behind. His parents thought He was traveling with their relatives or friends. But when evening came, Jesus wasn't with them. No one had seen Him, and Mary and Joseph became very worried. They hurried back to Jerusalem, hoping to find Him. It took them all the next day to get there. Early the following morning they found Him in the Temple, listening to the religious teachers and asking questions. All who heard

Him, including His parents, were amazed at His understanding of Scripture and the insightful answers He gave.

His mother motioned to Him to come to her and then asked, "Son, why did You stay behind? We've been looking for You everywhere. We were so scared that something had happened to You."

Jesus answered, "You should have known that I would be doing My Father's business." But His parents didn't fully understand.

Together they returned to Nazareth, and He obeyed them as before. His mother treasured every moment with Him and hid all these memories in her heart. Jesus continued to develop physically and to increase in wisdom, loved by God and all who knew Him (Luke 2:41-52).

two

Jesus Prepares for Ministry

In the fifteenth year of Tiberius Caesar, Pilate was governor of Judea, the son of Herod the Great ruled over the province of Galilee, and his brother Philip administered the adjoining two territories to the north and east. Annas and Caiphas were high priests in Jerusalem. Annas was semi-retired, and his son-in-law, Caiphas, was actually in charge.

During this time God directed John, who was living in the wilderness, to begin his ministry. So John started preaching by the Jordan River. He urged people to repent, turn from their sins, give their hearts to God, and be baptized.

Isaiah had predicted this when he said: "A voice will be heard in the wilderness, saying, 'Prepare the way for the Lord! Make His paths straight! Fill in the valleys! Level the hills! Straighten the curves and smooth the rough places! Then everyone will see the salvation of the Lord!'"

John often turned to the crowd and said, "Some of you are religious leaders, and people think you're harmless. But you're like snakes hiding in the grass, ready to strike. If you're so innocent, why are you here? Who warned you of God's judgment? Are you afraid something will happen to you? Turn from your sins and give your heart to God. Don't just say to yourselves, 'We're descendants of Abraham, so we're under God's protection.' Let me tell you—God can increase the family of Abraham by turning these stones into people. God will cut down all trees that don't bear fruit and will throw them into the fire, roots and all."

The people asked, "What should we do to get ready for the Messiah?"

John answered, "If you have two coats, give one to someone who doesn't have one. If you have food, share it with those who are hungry."

The tax collectors asked, "What should we do?"

John replied, "Stop collecting more taxes than the government requires and pocketing the rest."

Some of the soldiers asked, "What should we do?"

John said, "Don't be so violent. Don't accuse people of things they didn't do. Don't accept bribes. Be content with your pay."

John's preaching created such an expectation of the Messiah that some people wondered if John himself were the Messiah. John stated, "I'm just a preacher, and I baptize with water. But when the Messiah comes, He will baptize you with the Holy Spirit. He is so much greater than I am that I'm not even worthy to untie His sandals. He will separate the wheat from the weeds, store the wheat in His barn, and throw the weeds into the fire, where they'll all burn up."

In his preaching John spoke in ways that people could understand as he announced the coming of the Messiah (Luke 3:1-18).

Jesus Is Baptized

Jesus was about 30 years old when John started preaching and baptizing people in the Jordan River. His message was simple: "Repent and be baptized, because God is ready to set up His kingdom."

When Jesus heard that His cousin John was preaching and baptizing, He came down to Judea from Galilee to be baptized by John. When they met, John could sense Jesus' holiness and refused to baptize Him. He looked at Jesus and said, "I need to be baptized by You, so why are You coming to me?"

Jesus answered, "I want you to baptize Me because it's the right thing to do."

So John agreed and baptized Him. As soon as Jesus came up out of the water, heaven seemed to open, and the light of the Holy Spirit, shaped like a dove, hovered over Jesus' head. A voice from heaven said, "This is My beloved Son, with whom I am very pleased."

Jesus Is Tempted

Immediately the Holy Spirit led Jesus into the wilderness to prepare Him for His ministry. He was there for 40 days with wild animals all around, but angels were also there protecting Him. During this time He ate nothing. By the time His fast was over, He was extremely hungry. This was the devil's opportunity to tempt Him as never before.

Satan came to Jesus as an angel of light and said to Him, "If You are the Son of God, show Your power by changing these stones into bread."

Jesus responded, "One cannot live on bread alone, but must also feed on the Word of God."

Then the devil took Jesus to Jerusalem, set Him on the highest point of the Temple, and said, "If You are the Son of God, show Your faith in God's Word and jump off. The Scripture says: 'God will send His angels to care for you so that when you fall, they will catch you, and you won't even stub your foot against a stone.' "

Jesus responded, "The Scripture also says, 'Don't put the love of the Lord your God to a test.' "

Next the devil took Jesus to the peak of a very high mountain and gave Him a view of the world and the leisure that goes with power and wealth. Then he said, "I'll give You all of this. All You have to do is to kneel and bow to me."

Jesus responded, "Get behind Me, Satan. The Scripture says that this world belongs to God. Only before Him will I bow."

Then the devil left Him alone until a more convenient opportunity came to tempt Him again. Jesus was so weak that it looked as if He would die. But angels came to revive Him (Matt. 3:1, 2, 13-17; 4:1-11; Mark 1:13; Luke 3:21-23; 4:1-13).

three

Jesus Begins His Ministry

While Jesus was in the wilderness preparing for His ministry and being tempted by the devil, the Jewish leaders in Jerusalem decided to send a delegation of priests to the Jordan River to ask John whether he was the Messiah. John told them, "I am not." They asked, "Well, then, who are you? Are you Elijah come back from heaven?" John said, "No." They asked, "Are you that prophet Moses said would come to help us?" Again John said, "No." They persisted, "Then who are you? Tell us so we can take an answer back to those who sent us. Speak up. What do you have to say for yourself?" John quoted the words of Isaiah: "I am just a voice crying in the wilderness, 'Prepare the way of the Lord. Make a highway for our God.'"

The priests would not give up and pressed John for an answer to take back to Jerusalem. "So if you're not the Messiah or Elijah or that prophet that Moses spoke about, why are you out here preaching and baptizing people?" John answered, "I baptize only with water, but there is Someone in the crowd you don't know. He will soon begin His ministry and is the one who will change people's lives. I'm not worthy to unfasten His sandals." Now all this happened near Bethany on the other side of the Jordan River.

The next day when John saw Jesus coming through the crowd toward him, he pointed to Him and called out, "Look! There He is, the Lamb of God who takes away sin! This is the one I've been telling you about. He existed before I was born, and has the power and authority to change your hearts. I didn't know He was the one when He came to be baptized. But when God asked me to preach and baptize, He said, 'When you see the light of the Holy Spirit coming down from heaven and remain on someone, that is the one who will baptize people with the Holy Spirit.' I'm telling you the truth of what I heard and saw. This is the one I'm pointing out to you. He is the Messiah, the Son of God" (John 1:19-34).

21

Jesus Begins Choosing Disciples

The following morning as John was talking to two of his disciples, he saw Jesus walking among the people. "Look!" he said, "There He is! The Lamb of God!" The two disciples looked to where John was pointing, left him, and followed Jesus through the crowd. When they caught up with Him, Jesus turned and said, "Why are you following Me? What do you want?" They said, "Sir, where are You staying? We would like to talk to You. May we follow You home?" Jesus said, "Come along and see." They followed Him to where He was staying and talked with Him that whole day until late that afternoon.

One of the two who had followed Jesus that day was Andrew, Peter's brother. The first thing Andrew did was to find his brother and say to him, "Simon, we have found the Messiah! Come, let me take you to Him." When Jesus met Simon, he said, "I'm glad to meet you. From now on you'll be called Peter."

The next day Jesus headed north to Galilee. On the way He saw Philip and said, "Come, follow Me." Philip was from Bethsaida, Peter and Andrew's hometown. First Philip rushed off to find his friend Nathaniel. When he found him, he said, "Nathaniel! We have found Him, the one Moses and the prophets wrote about! His name is Jesus, the son of Joseph, the carpenter in Nazareth." Nathaniel responded, "Nazareth? How can anything good come out of that place?" Philip said, "Come and see for yourself."

So Nathaniel followed Philip, and when Jesus met him, he said, "A true Israelite. There's not a dishonest bone in your body." Nathaniel said, "How do you know so much about me?" Jesus answered, "Before Philip found you, I saw you sitting under a fig tree praying." Nathaniel responded, "Sir, You must be the Messiah, the Son of God, the promised King of Israel!" Jesus looked at him and said, "Because I said, 'I saw you sitting under a fig tree praying,' is that why you believe who I am? Soon you will see and hear many more things to strengthen your faith, and you will know that heaven has opened its doors and that angels are going back and forth helping Me to carry out My mission" (John 1:35-51).

Jesus' First Miracle

Three days later Jesus and His disciples attended a wedding in the little town of Cana in Galilee.

There were so many people there that during that the festivities the family ran out of wine. So Jesus' mother told Him the problem. Jesus answered, "Mother, I respect you, but this is not the time for Me to work a miracle unless God tells Me to." Mary understood, and in faith she said to the servants, "Whatever my Son asks you to do, do it."

Nearby there were six large water jars that could hold about 30 gallons of water each. Jesus said to the servants, "Fill these water jars to the top. Then dip some out and take it to the master of ceremonies to taste." They did what He said, and when they dipped out what they thought was water, they found that it was freshly made wine. When the master of ceremonies tasted it, he didn't ask where it came from, but went to the bridegroom and said, "You know that at a wedding party you serve the best-tasting drink first. When everyone is full, then you serve the less-expensive drinks. But you have kept the best until last."

This was the first of many miracles that Jesus did during His ministry. When the disciples saw this, they were more convinced than ever that Jesus was the long-awaited Messiah. After the wedding, Jesus went with His mother, stepbrothers, and disciples to Capernaum by the lake to rest for a few days.

Jesus Cleanses the Temple

Soon it was time to celebrate the annual Passover. So Jesus and His disciples, along with many others, made their way to Jerusalem. The Temple court was filled with people and merchants buying and selling young oxen, sheep, goats, and pigeons for sacrifices. Others were exchanging money for the proper coins to pay the Temple tax.

When Jesus saw all this, His spirit was so stirred that He picked up pieces of discarded rope, made them into a whip, and asked the merchants and money changers to leave. When they refused, He tipped over their tables, opened the pigeon cages, and said, "Get out and take your animals with you. I will not let you turn My Father's house into a marketplace!" The disciples witnessing all this remembered the prophecy about the Messiah that said: "The zeal for God's house is eating me up."

The Jewish leaders didn't like what they saw. They demanded of Jesus, "What right do You have to do such a thing? If you think You're doing God's work, then perform a miracle, as Moses did for our ancestors to show that God had sent him." Jesus saw nothing but hatred in their eyes. He looked at them and said, "Destroy this temple, and in three days I'll rebuild it." They responded, "It took 46 years to make this Temple what it is today, and You're telling us that You could do it in three days?" Jesus was talking about His body as a temple, but they thought He was talking about the Temple they were in. After He was raised from the dead, the disciples remembered what He had said that day in the Temple, and their faith in the prophecies and in what He had taught them became even stronger.

This happened at the beginning of Jesus' ministry at the Passover in Jerusalem. Many people already believed that He was the Messiah because of the miracles He had done, and His zeal for the Temple convinced them even more. But Jesus didn't trust the crowd, because He knew how changeable human nature can be. No one ever needed to tell Him what people were thinking, because He always knew (John 2).

four

Jesus' Concern for Others

Now there was a highly respected leader of the Jewish High Council named Nicodemus. He wanted to talk to Jesus privately, so he came to see Him at night. "Teacher," he said, "we know that God has sent You, because no one could work such miracles as You have unless God is with him."

Jesus responded, "Miracles are not enough on which to hang your faith. You must be born again."

This surprised Nicodemus, so he asked, "How can a man be born a second time? That's impossible. He would have to get back into his mother's womb."

Jesus replied, "I'm talking about spiritual birth. No one can belong to the kingdom of God unless he is changed by the power of the Holy Spirit and is willing to be baptized. Don't be shocked by what I'm saying, because being born again is beyond human logic and is not the result of some religious ritual. It's like the wind. You can hear it and see the effects of it, but you can't see the wind itself. You can't tell where it began or where it will end up. In the same way, you can't explain how people are born again or point to something and say, 'This is what did it.'"

Nicodemus was stunned. Finally he spoke: "I still don't understand. How can this be?"

Jesus said, "You mean you're a religious leader and don't understand what I'm saying? I'm telling you what I know and what I've seen, and yet you don't believe Me. If you can't understand with an illustration from everyday life, how can you understand if I tell you what's going on in heaven? No one has lived in heaven and then come to live here except the One who is talking to you. Just as Moses put a bronze serpent on a pole and held it up for the people to look at and be healed from a snakebite, so the Son of Man must be put on a cross and held up for everyone to see. Those who look and believe will be healed from the snakebite of sin and be given eternal life."

Jesus continued: "For God so loved the world that He gave His only Son to come and die so that whoever believes in Him will not perish but will be given eternal life. God did not send His Son to this world to condemn people, but to save them. There is no judgment against those who believe in God's Son and accept Him as their Savior, but those who don't believe in Him will be judged. What judges people is the light of heaven that has come into the world, but some love darkness more than light because their deeds are evil. Those who do what is good gladly turn to the light, and it will be clearly seen that God has been working in their lives" (John 3:1-21).

Jesus and John

After the interview with Nicodemus, Jesus decided to leave Jerusalem but to stay in Judea and let His disciples preach and baptize. John was preaching and baptizing near Salim because the Jordan River was deeper there. This was before Herod arrested John and put him in prison.

Now some of John's disciples had been arguing with the priests about the importance of baptism and ceremonial cleansing. When they heard that Jesus' disciples were preaching and baptizing nearby, they went to John and said, "The One you say is the Messiah is letting His disciples preach and baptize, and a lot of people are going there!"

John responded, "God appointed me to prepare the way for Him. It is like what takes place at a wedding. The bride belongs to the bridegroom, but the bridegroom's friend stands by and is happy for him. That's how it is with me. I'm His friend. He must increase, but I must decrease.

"He has come down from above. I'm from here on earth. He can tell you about heavenly things because He was there. I can't, because my understanding is limited. I can tell you only about things here. Yet so few believe what He says. But there are those who believe what He says because of what God said about Him in Scripture. He teaches with conviction because the power of the Holy Spirit has been given to Him without measure. The Father loves Him and has given Him authority over everything down here. So all who believe in Him already have eternal life implanted in their hearts. Those who refuse to believe in Him will not be given eternal life and will have to face God's judgment on sin."

When Jesus heard that John's disciples were upset over the large number of people that Jesus was baptizing—although Jesus Himself baptized no one (His disciples did the baptizing)—and that the Pharisees were concerned over His rising popularity, He decided to leave Judea and return to Galilee (John 3:22-36; 4:1-3).

Jesus and the Samaritan Woman

On the way north to Galilee, Jesus had to go through the province of Samaria. At noon He stopped to rest at a well near the village of Sychar. This was the land that Jacob had given to his son Joseph, and the well was named "Jacob's Well."

When a Samaritan woman came to draw water from the well, Jesus said to her, "After you draw your water, please let Me have a drink. I am so thirsty." He was alone when this happened because His disciples had gone into the village to buy some food.

The woman was surprised and responded, "You're a Jew, and You're asking a Samaritan woman for a drink of water? You Jews would rather die than to have anything to do with us."

Jesus answered, "If you only knew how much God loves you and who I am, you would be asking Me for a drink of living water, and I would give it to you."

The woman said, "Sir, this well is very deep, and You don't have a rope or a bucket. So how are You going to draw water to give me a drink? This is Jacob's well. He and his sons and his cattle drank from it. This is what makes it so special."

Jesus said, "This is a special well and it has good water, but after people drink it they get thirsty again. If you drink the water I'm talking about, you'll never be thirsty again. It will be like a spring inside of you bubbling up to eternal life."

The woman exclaimed, "That's the kind of water I need! Then I won't have to come here to haul water ever again, because I'll never get thirsty."

Jesus said, "Go and bring your husband, and I'll give this water to both of you."

The woman replied, "I don't have a husband."

Jesus answered, "I know. You've been married five times, and the man you're living with now is not your husband."

The woman gasped, "How do you know all this about me? You must be a prophet! So tell me, why is it that you Jews insist that you have the true religion and that Jerusalem is the only place to worship God? Our ancestors worshiped in their own way on this mountain for centuries."

Jesus answered, "The time is coming when Jerusalem will be destroyed and it won't matter where you worship. But salvation will come through the Jews. Aside from that, true worship is a matter of the heart and spirit, not so much where it is done. These are the kinds of worshippers the Father is looking for, and this is what really matters. God is a spiritual being, so those who worship Him must worship Him in spirit and in truth."

The woman replied, "I don't understand everything You're saying. All I know is that when the Messiah comes, the one who is called the Christ, He will explain everything to us and tell us what's right."

Jesus said, "I am the Messiah."

Just then the disciples returned and were shocked to see Jesus talking to a Samaritan woman, but none of them asked Him why He had done so or what they had talked about. The woman sensed that she was not welcome, so she left her water bucket and ran back to the village and told everyone she met, "Come and see a stranger who talks like a prophet. He knows everything I've ever done. I think He's the Messiah!"

Meanwhile, the disciples urged Jesus to eat, saying, "Master, we know You're hungry. Have something to eat."

Jesus insisted, "I have food that you don't know about. I've been eating all the time you've been gone."

The disciples asked each other, "Maybe someone brought Him food while we were in town."

Jesus said, "The food I'm talking about is the satisfaction that comes from doing God's work and seeing this woman respond. When we talk about harvesting, don't think about earthly harvests and say, 'In four months it will be harvesttime.' Spiritually it's always harvesttime. Just look around you, and you'll see how people are longing for God and are ready to be harvested. God will pay His harvesters for what they have done, and the fruit they harvest is people for eternal life. Then those who sow and those who reap will rejoice together when they see the fruit of their labor. The old saying 'Some sow and others reap' is true. I'm sending you out to harvest what others have sowed. In that sense you're already working together."

When the woman told the people about Jesus, many believed what she said and went out to see the man who claimed to be the Messiah. They begged Him to stay with them. He agreed, and remained in their village for two days. And when the people heard Him, many more believed. They said to the woman, "We believe Him to be the Messiah, not because of what you told us, but because we have listened to Him ourselves. Without a doubt He is the Christ, the Savior of the world!" (John 4:1-42).

Jesus Helps a Government Official

After two days in Samaria, Jesus continued His way north into Galilee and on to Nazareth, even though He knew that a prophet received more respect elsewhere than in his own hometown. When He crossed the border into Galilee, the people were glad to see Him because many had seen Him work miracles at the Passover in Jerusalem.

On the way to Nazareth, Jesus decided to stop at the village of Cana, where He had worked His first miracle at a wedding feast. A nobleman from the king's court lived in nearby Capernaum. When he heard that Jesus was in Cana, he hurried to see Him.

When he found Jesus, he asked Him to heal his little son, who was at the point of death. Jesus responded, "Must I work a miracle so that you and your people will believe in Me?"

The government official answered, "Lord, forgive me. But please come and heal my son or he will die."

Jesus said, "Go back home—your son is healed."

The official believed Jesus and started for home. He was so confident that his son had been healed that he took his time. As he neared home, his servants noticed him approaching and ran to meet him with the good news, saying, "Master, your little son is alive!"

He asked them when the boy began getting better.

They replied, "Yesterday about one o'clock in the afternoon his fever suddenly left him!"

The official knew that this was the exact time Jesus had said, "Go back home—your son is healed." When he told his family how he had met Jesus and about their conversation, they all believed.

This was the second great miracle that Jesus did in the little town of Cana at the beginning of His ministry (John 4:43-54).

Jesus Goes Back Home

From Cana Jesus decided to return to Nazareth, where He had grown up. Along the way, He preached in the synagogues and on the streets. The Holy Spirit was with Him, and throughout the whole area those who heard Him were happy for what He did and said.

When He reached Nazareth, He went to the synagogue on the Sabbath as He always did. The leader of the synagogue welcomed Him, handed Him the scroll of Isaiah, and asked Him to read a passage of Scripture. Jesus unrolled the scroll to the place where it said, "The power of the Spirit is upon me because the Lord has anointed me to preach the good news of salvation to the poor, to heal broken hearts, to deliver people from the power of sin, to open the eyes of the blind, to bring liberty to the oppressed, and to proclaim the year of the Lord's promise."

Jesus rolled up the scroll, gave it to the synagogue official, and sat down. Everyone was spellbound by the way He had read the scripture, and they just kept looking at Him. Then He said, "This scripture is being fulfilled before your very eyes." The people were amazed at His gracious ways and how well He spoke. And they all quietly praised Him.

Then someone said, "Isn't this Joseph's son? He grew up here. So how can He apply this prophecy to Himself?"

Jesus responded, "You'll probably quote the proverb, 'A physician must first heal himself before people will come to him.' This means you want Me to work the same miracles here that I've worked in Capernaum before you'll believe Me. How true it is that a prophet is not accepted in his own hometown!

"Look what happened in the days of Elijah. There were many widows in Israel who needed help during that 3 ½-year drought. But God sent Elijah to a widow in Zarephath in the land of Sidon to help her. Or what about Elisha? He healed Naaman, an officer of the king of Syria, rather than the lepers in Israel."

When the people heard Jesus say that non-Israelites had more faith than they had, their praise turned to anger. They grabbed Him and dragged Him through the streets to the edge of a cliff at the city's edge, intending to push Him over. But when they got there, He freed Himself and quietly walked through the crowd and went on His way (Luke 4:14-30).

While Jesus was in Galilee, John was still preaching and teaching in Judea. He told the people that Herod had done wrong in taking his half brother Philip's wife Herodias and marrying her, and John described all the other evil things that the ruler had done. John had also told Herod this privately. When Herod heard what John was saying, he had him arrested and put in prison, adding this sin to his many others (Mark 6:17, 18; Luke 3:19, 20).

five

Jesus Expands His Ministry

After the people in Nazareth turned against Jesus, He decided to make Capernaum His hometown. This is what the prophet Isaiah had predicted when he said: "The people living by the Sea of Galilee will be blessed. They will no longer live in darkness, but will see great light, and that light will give them hope."

From that time on, Jesus began preaching and teaching like John the Baptist, saying, "Repent and change your ways, for the kingdom of God is here" (Matt. 4:13-17).

One day as Jesus was teaching on the shore of the Lake of Galilee, the crowd became quite large and the people pressed in to hear what He had to say, so much so that they almost pushed Him into the water. Jesus noticed two empty fishing boats and some fishermen standing in the shallow water washing their nets. He stepped into the boat belonging to Peter and asked him to push a little off shore. Then He sat down and taught the people from there.

When He finished, He said to Peter, "Row out to where it's deep and throw out your nets."

As he rowed, Peter said, "Master, we fished all night and didn't catch a thing. During the day the fish go way down where it's cool and dark. But if You say so, we'll do it."

Then Peter and his men threw out their nets. They caught so many fish that when they pulled in their nets, they started to break. So they shouted to James and John to bring their boat to help them. They filled both boats with so many fish that they almost sank.

Then Peter fell on his knees in front of Jesus, who was sitting in the boat, and said, "Lord, I'm a sinful man! Why do You even bother with me?" He and all who were with him were awestruck by this huge catch of fish in the middle of the day, as were James and John.

Jesus said to Peter, "Don't be so surprised, and don't be afraid of

Me. From now on I want you to fish for people" (Luke 5:1-10).

Later as Jesus was walking along the shore, He saw Peter and his brother Andrew stretching out their nets by the lake, getting ready to fish again. He called to them, "Come, follow Me! I'll teach you how to fish for people!" Without hesitation Peter and Andrew left their nets with their workers and followed Him. Then Jesus saw James and John sitting in their father's boat mending nets. Jesus called to them, "Come, follow Me! I'll teach you how to use the net to fish for people!" Without hesitation they got up, left their father and the workers, and followed Him (Mark 1:16-20).

Jesus Heals on Sabbath

Together with His new disciples, Jesus went into town to heal and teach. The people of Capernaum were amazed at His teachings. He spoke with decided authority and yet so kindly and lovingly, not at all like the scribes and Pharisees and teachers of religious law. And every Sabbath Jesus and His disciples attended the synagogue.

One particular Sabbath a man present was demon-possessed. He stood up and shouted at Jesus, "Why are You bothering us? Leave us alone! You're Jesus from Nazareth. Have You come to destroy us? I know who You are. You're the Holy One sent from God!"

Jesus commanded the demon, "Be quiet and come out of the man."

The evil spirit screamed, threw the man down into convulsions, and, with a shriek, left him. The people were awestruck and said to themselves, "What kind of teacher is this? He speaks with such authority that even demons obey Him!"

News of what Jesus had done quickly spread throughout Galilee.

After leaving the synagogue, Jesus and the four disciples went to Peter's house. They found Peter's mother-in-law sick with a very high fever. When they told Jesus, He went into her room, gently took her hand, and helped her sit up. Immediately the fever left her. She got up and helped prepare the meal.

That evening after sunset the townspeople brought their sick and demon-possessed to Peter's house for Jesus to heal. Late into the night He healed the sick of all kinds of diseases, and cast out demons from many of them. As the demons came out, they shouted, "You are the Son of God!" because they knew who Jesus was. So He ordered them to be quiet and leave, and they did.

The next morning Jesus awoke long before daybreak and went up into the hills to a secluded place to pray. At daybreak Peter and the other disciples began looking for Him. When they found Him, they said, "People are already at the house asking for You."

Jesus replied, "I must preach the good news of salvation and help people in other towns as well. I wasn't sent only to the people of Capernaum, but to spread the message of the kingdom as far and wide as possible." And that's what He did.

Near one little town a leper came to Jesus, knelt in front of Him, and said, "I know that if You want to, You can heal me."

Jesus was moved with compassion for the man. So He reached out and touched him and said, "Of course I want to; be clean. Go on your way—you are healed. But you need to show yourself to the priests and let them pronounce you clean before going home. You need to carry out the appropriate ritual that Moses gave for lepers as a witness to the whole community that you are healed, so that all of them will welcome you home."

But the man did not go to the priests. Instead, on the way home he simply told everyone he met that Jesus had healed him.

This upset the priests, because the man had bypassed them and gone directly home. What the man had done greatly restricted Jesus' ministry so that He couldn't move as freely throughout the city as He had before. So He left and carried on His ministry of preaching and healing in small towns and isolated places. But before long, people found Him and came to Him from all over Galilee, the Ten Cities, Judea, Jerusalem, and even from as far north as Syria (Mark 1:21-45; Matt. 4:23-25).

Jesus Heals a Paralyzed Man

Sometime later Jesus returned to Capernaum, and the news spread that He was back in town. Soon the house where He was staying was so full of visitors that people outside crowded around the open windows to hear what He was saying.

Four men arrived carrying a paralyzed man on a mat, hoping to see Jesus and have Him heal their friend, but they couldn't get near the house. Determined, they pushed through part of the crowd, climbed up on the flat roof, and pulled the paralyzed man up after them. Then they took off a section of the roof and lowered their friend down right in front of Jesus.

This caught everyone's attention, and they wondered what Jesus would say. He praised the faith of these men, then looked in sympathy at the paralyzed man lying on the mat in front of him. "Son," he said, "don't be troubled—your sins are forgiven."

When the Pharisees and religious teachers heard that, each one said to himself, "That's blasphemy! Who does He think He is? Only God can forgive sins!"

Jesus knew what they were thinking and responded, "Why do you think what I said was blasphemy? Is it easier to say to a paralyzed man, 'Your sins are forgiven,' or 'Get up, roll up your mat, and go home'? To let you know that the Son of Man has authority on earth to forgive sins," He said as He turned back to the paralyzed man, "get up, roll up your mat, and go home."

Instantly the man's body responded. He rose to his feet, rolled up his mat, and walked through the crowd toward home. The people were stunned. Then they praised God and said, "Never have we seen anything like this!" (Mark 2:1-12).

Jesus and Matthew

Then Jesus thanked His host and made His way down to the lake, with crowds of people following Him. His plan was to lead them to a more open area by the shore and teach them there.

On the way He passed a public tax booth where Matthew was sitting, collecting taxes. Jesus stopped and said, "Come and follow Me." Matthew got up and followed Him.

A few days later Matthew invited Jesus and the other disciples to his home for dinner. He also invited some of his friends and fellow tax collectors, whom the Jews considered to be terrible sinners. Many of these people had been among the crowds following Jesus.

When the Pharisees and religious teachers found out that Jesus had agreed to eat with such people, they followed Him to Matthew's house. On the way they asked the disciples, "How can your Master eat with such people as these Jewish tax collectors, who work for the Romans, and with others who live in open sin?"

Jesus overheard their conversation and answered, "People who are healthy don't need a physician—only people who are sick. I've come to help people who are convicted of sin and know they need God, not those who think they're already good enough."

After Jesus reached Matthew's house, these same religious teachers asked Jesus, "Why are Your disciples always feasting instead of fasting twice a week, as John's disciples do?"

Jesus responded with a question: "Do wedding guests fast when they're sitting at the table with the bridegroom? After the bridegroom leaves and the wedding party is over, there will be time enough to fast" (Mark 2:13-20).

Jesus and the Sabbath

One Sabbath morning, as Jesus and His disciples were walking through a grainfield, they stopped and broke off some heads of grain. After rubbing them in their hands, they ate them, because they were hungry. Some Pharisees came along, and when they saw this, they said to Jesus,

"Don't You realize that Your disciples are harvesting on the Sabbath? That's breaking the law!"

Jesus said, "Really? Haven't you read in Scripture what David did when he and his men were hungry and in need? He went to the sanctuary to see the high priest and asked for something to eat. The high priest gave him the only thing he had on hand, the ceremonial bread set aside for the Lord, which only priests were allowed to eat. He gave David enough for himself and his men.

"It's the same with the Sabbath. God gave the Sabbath to help us, not to enslave us. I know what's right to do on the Sabbath and what isn't. The Son of Man is Lord of the Sabbath."

On another Sabbath, when Jesus went to the synagogue, a man with a deformed hand was there. The scribes and Pharisees watched Jesus to see if He would heal the man so they could accuse Him of breaking the Sabbath. Jesus knew what they were thinking. So He motioned to the man to come up front, which he did. Then Jesus turned to His critics and said, "Let Me ask you a question. Which is better—to do good on the Sabbath, or to think evil? Is it lawful to heal someone on the Sabbath or to let them suffer?"

While they were figuring out how to answer Him, Jesus turned to the man and said, "Hold out your deformed hand." The man did, and instantly his hand was restored. When the scribes and Pharisees saw what Jesus had done, they were filled with rage and immediately plotted with the Herodians how to get rid of Him (Mark 2:23-28; 3:1-6).

Jesus Goes to Jerusalem

Sometime later Jesus decided to leave Galilee and make His way to Jerusalem for the Passover. Not far from the Temple was the Sheep Gate, and nearby, the Pool of Bethesda. It was surrounded by a covered walkway with columns and arches. Hundreds of sick people—blind, limping, partially paralyzed—came there, waiting for the mysterious moving of the water. They sat or laid on mats, believing that periodically an angel came to disturb the quiet water and the first one in afterward would be healed.

One of the men lying there had been paralyzed for 38 years. When Jesus learned how long he had been that way, He asked him, "Would you like to be healed?"

The man answered, "How can I, when no one helps me into the water at the right time? When I try to get in on my own, someone always gets there before I do."

Jesus responded, "Stand up, roll up your mat, and walk!" The man put forth the effort and was healed. He stood up, rolled up his mat, and walked away.

This happened on the Sabbath. When the Jewish leaders saw the man walking along carrying his mat, they stopped him and said, "Today is the Sabbath. You're not allowed to carry your mat. It's against the law."

He answered, "The man who healed me told me to roll up my mat and go home."

They asked, "Who told you to do that?"

The man didn't know, because while he was rolling up his mat, Jesus had slipped away into the crowd.

Later Jesus saw the man in the Temple thanking God for healing him. Jesus walked over to him and said, "It's good to see you well. Don't go back to a life of sinning, or you might end up with something worse."

The man recognized Jesus and went and told the religious leaders that it was Jesus who had healed him. When the authorities heard this, they determined to have Jesus arrested and executed for Sabbathbreaking. But when they questioned Him about what He had done, Jesus replied, "My Father never stops working for people, and neither do I."

This made the Jewish leaders more determined than ever to find a way to kill Him, not only because He broke their Sabbath rules but because He said that God was His Father, making Himself equal with God.

Jesus continued, "I don't do anything independently from My Father. I do only what My Father says. He tells Me what to do, and I do it. The Father loves the Son and includes Him in everything. Soon the Son will do even greater miracles than healing a man. You'll be amazed because you will see Me raise the dead just as the Father does. The Father is not your judge. He condemns no one, but has entrusted the judgment of the world to the Son so that everyone will honor the Son as they honor the Father. Those who do not honor the Son do not honor the Father who sent Him.

"I tell you a solemn truth: Those who listen to what I say and believe that God has sent Me will not be condemned for their sins, but will be forgiven and will receive eternal life. The time is coming, and in one sense is already here, when the dead will hear My voice and live. Just as the Father is the giver of life, so is the Son. He has given Him authority to judge the whole world because He is the Son of Man.

"The time is coming when all who are dead will hear My voice. Those who have done good will rise and be given eternal life, but those who have done wickedly will rise to be condemned and to perish. I do nothing without consulting the Father. My judgment is just and fair because I don't do as I please—I do what pleases the Father who sent Me.

"In a courtroom, if only one witness speaks in favor of someone, it doesn't count. There must be at least two. What John the Baptist said about Me is true. However, the best witness is not from John, even though I draw your attention to what he said. John was a shining light in Israel, and for a while you were pleased with his ministry. But My ministry with its miracles is the other witness. It's My Father's witness. Can't you see what God is doing through My ministry and hear what He is saying? The reason you can't is that you don't take what I say seriously. You think you take the Scriptures seriously, and you study them diligently because you believe they will give you eternal life. But their very words testify of Me. Yet you're not willing to believe in Me and receive eternal life.

"Your approval or disapproval of what I do is not that important to me. The problem is that you don't really love God, no matter what you say. I've come to show you the Father, but you refuse to accept Me, no matter what I say or do. If someone else came and claimed to speak for God, saying what you like to hear, you would accept him. No wonder you can't accept Me. You love to honor each other, but you're not concerned about honoring God.

"I'm not here to accuse you before the Father. Moses, in whom you place your confidence and hope, will do that. If you really believed Moses, you would believe Me, because he wrote about Me. But if you don't believe what he said, how can you believe what I say?" (John 5).

six

By the Lake and on the Hillside

W/hen Jesus returned to Galilee, a huge crowd followed Him and His disciples to the lake. Many had come up from Judea and from as far away as Tyre and Sidon. They had heard about the miracles Jesus had done, and they wanted to see for themselves.

When Jesus saw all these people, He told His disciples to get a boat ready in case He was crowded off the beach. He healed a number of people. Then they crowded around Him, trying so hard to touch Him that they almost pushed Him into the water. Those who were demon-possessed fell down in front of Him, shrieking, "You are the Son of God! Yes, You are!"

Jesus ordered them to stop their shrieking, and they did. He did not want them to be the cause of a disturbance that would cut short His ministry.

Later that day Jesus decided to leave the lake and climb a nearby hill, taking with Him those whom He had chosen to be His disciples. When they were alone, He set them apart as apostles. There were 12 of them: Peter and his brother Andrew, James and his brother John, Philip, Bartholomew (also called Nathaniel), Matthew, Thomas, James the younger, Thaddaeus, Simon the patriot, and Judas, who later betrayed him (Mark 3:7-19).

Sermon on the Mount—1

On another day so many people were crowding around Jesus that He decided to go out of town to a hillside where there was plenty of room. He sat on the hill surrounded by His disciples, blessed the people, and began teaching them the values of the kingdom.

"Blessed are those who feel their need of God; the kingdom of heaven is already inside of them. Blessed are those who feel bad when they sin and ask God to forgive them; they will be forgiven and comforted. Blessed are those who are gentle and who gladly listen to God; the whole earth will someday belong to them. Blessed are those who long for justice and do what's right; they will be rewarded. Blessed are those who are merciful and kind; they will receive mercy and kindness. Blessed are those whose hearts are pure; the day is coming when they will see God face to face. Blessed are the peacemakers; they are doing heaven's work and are God's children. Blessed are those who are poor in this world's goods; God will give them the riches of His kingdom. Blessed are those who don't have enough food and are hungry; they will eat from the tree of life and be satisfied. Blessed are those who mourn; God will wipe away their tears, and they will laugh for joy. Blessed are those who suffer for doing what is right; they belong to the kingdom of heaven. When people laugh at you, lie about you, and persecute you, don't get discouraged. A great reward awaits you in heaven, along with the prophets who were treated like that before you (Matt. 5:1–9; Luke 6:20, 21; Matt. 5:10-12).

"I feel sorry for those who are rich and think only of money; their only happiness is now. I feel sorry for those who overindulge and think of little else but feasting; their only satisfaction is now. I feel sorry for those who live for pleasure and think of nothing but entertainment; their only joy is now. I feel sorry for those who live only to be well spoken of by others. I feel sorry for those who love to hear only smooth things and praise false prophets as their fathers did" (Luke 6:24-26).

Sermon on the Mount—2

Jesus went on to say, "You are the salt of the earth. But what good is salt if it loses its taste? It's good for nothing, so people throw it out.

"You are the light of the world, like a city on a hill lighting up the night sky. People don't light a lamp and then cover it up, but set it on a lampstand so that everyone in the house can see. In the same way, let your light shine by helping others and doing good. People will thank God for you and praise your heavenly Father for what you have done for them.

"I want you to know why I have come. I did not come to do away with what Moses and the prophets wrote. I came to fulfill what they said. I'm telling you the truth: As long as there is heaven and earth, not the smallest stroke of a pen will be erased from what is written until everything is carried out."

Then Jesus explained the deeper meaning of God's law. "Moses told you not to kill, and if you do, you will be taken before a judge and given the death penalty. But I say to you, Whoever has murder in his heart is guilty of breaking the law and is subject to God's judgment.

"If you curse people, you'll be answerable to the Jewish High Court. But if you look down on people and call them names, you are on your way to destruction. If you come to the Temple with your offering and remember that you need to make things right with someone, go and do it. Then come and give God your offering. If you are being sued, settle out of court. Do it quickly, even if it's on the way to court. Once you stand before the judge, he may have you thrown into prison until you can pay.

"Moses told you not to break an oath but to keep every promise you make to God. Now don't confirm with an oath everything you promise to do, swearing by heaven or by something on earth, because you're not the one in charge—God is. And don't swear by Jerusalem, because it's governed by the king. Don't even swear by yourself, because you can't change the color of even your hair. Just say yes or no and keep your word. Don't confirm everything you promise to do with an oath. People will think something is wrong and will not really trust you.

"Moses also said that it is right and just for victims to demand that the same be done to a criminal that he did to them, such as an 'eye for an eye' and a 'tooth for a tooth.' But don't demand equal justice for every little thing. If someone slaps you on one cheek, don't retaliate and slap back. Be willing to let that person slap you on the other cheek, too. If someone threatens to sue and take your coat, give that person your shirt as well. If a Roman soldier forces you to carry his pack one mile, carry it for two miles. Show a helpful spirit, no matter how you feel. If someone asks for help, help that person. If someone wants to borrow something, lend it to that individual.

"You have been taught to love your neighbors and hate your enemies. You should love both your neighbors and your enemies. Pray for them and for those who turn against you. That will show that you're becoming like your heavenly Father, who makes the sun to shine on both those who love Him and those who don't. He waters the crops of the righteous and the wicked. If you love only those who love you, how does that differ from the unrighteous? If you greet only a brother who greets you, or speak only to those who speak to you, how does that differ from what unbelievers do? Be generous and full of love, like your Father in heaven" (Matt. 5:13-48).

Sermon on the Mount—3

Jesus continued: "Don't do good things so that you can be praised and admired by others. If you do, you already have your reward. Your Father in heaven can't give you another reward. When you help someone in need, don't tell everyone about it, as the Pharisees do—not even your friends. When you help others, do it quietly and without show. Don't let your left hand know what your right hand is doing. Your heavenly Father sees what you do and will reward you for it.

"And when you pray, don't be like the Pharisees. They love to pray loudly in the synagogue and on street corners so that people will notice them. They have their reward. When you pray, go where you can be alone, close the door, and quietly pray to your heavenly Father. He will hear your prayers and reward you for it. When you pray, don't keep saying the same thing again and again. That's what unbelievers do. They think their prayers are being heard because of the repetitions. Don't pray that way. Your heavenly Father knows your needs before you even ask.

"When you pray, say something like this: Our heavenly Father, may Your name be honored in all that we do. May we extend Your kingdom. May Your will be done on earth as it is in heaven. Provide us with our daily food. Forgive us as we forgive those who sin against us. Help us not to give in to temptation, but deliver us from the evil one. For Yours is the kingdom, the power, and the glory, forever. Amen.

"If you forgive others, your heavenly Father will forgive you. But if you don't forgive others, your heavenly Father can't forgive you.

"When you fast, don't make it as obvious as the Pharisees do, who try to look pale and sad so that people will admire them. When you fast, comb your hair, wash your face, and look happy. That way no one will know you're fasting except your heavenly Father, who knows everything you do. He will reward you for it.

"Don't store up treasures here on earth, where moths and rust destroy things, and where thieves break in and steal. Store up your treasure in heaven, where it's safe from moths and rust and thieves. Where your money is, that's where your heart will be also.

"The same priority applies to your eyes. If they look at what is good, you will be filled with goodness and light. If they look at what is bad, you will be filled with darkness and evil. If your heart is dark, things look dark everywhere.

"You can't serve two masters. Either you will hate one and love the other, or you'll devote yourself to one and despise the other. You can't serve God and money at the same time.

"Don't worry about the things of this life—what you're going to eat or wear. Life is more important than food and clothes. Look at the birds: They don't plant, harvest, or store their food in barns, because your heavenly Father feeds them. You are so much more valuable than birds. Besides, you can't add one extra hour to your life by worrying. So why worry about the clothes that you're going to wear? Look at the flowers of the field and how they grow. They don't worry about what to wear, yet Solomon in all his glory was not dressed as beautifully as they are. If God cares about flowers, which are here today and cut down tomorrow, how much more does He care about you! You have such little faith.

"Don't worry so much about food and clothes. That's the first thing unbelievers think about. Your heavenly Father knows what you need. Make His kingdom and righteousness first in your life, and the necessities of life will be met as well. So don't worry about what may or may not happen tomorrow, because tomorrow will have its own concerns. Carry your responsibilities one day at a time.

"Stop judging others. The standards you apply to them, God will apply to you. The measuring line you use on others will be used on you. Why do you keep looking at the speck of sawdust in your brother's eye and can't see the log in your own eye? How can you say to him, 'Hold still while I get this speck of sawdust out of your eye,' when you have a log in your own eye? First take the log out of your own eye; then you'll see things more clearly and be able to help get the speck out of your brother's eye.

"Don't try to share holy things with people who don't want to listen. It's like throwing pearls to pigs. They'll trample them in the mud and then turn on you.

"When you pray, keep on asking, and you will receive what is best for you. Keep on looking, and you will find what you need. Keep on knocking, and the door will open for you. Everyone who asks, receives; everyone who seeks, finds; and for everyone who knocks, the door will open.

"Which of you parents will give a stone to your son when he asks for a piece of bread? Or will parents give a snake to a child who asks for a fish? If sinful people give good things to their children, how much more will your heavenly Father give good things to those who ask Him! So be good to others, just as you would have them be good to you. This is what God's law and the Scriptures are all about.

"You can't get into God's kingdom by following the crowd. The road to destruction is broad and the gate is wide, and lots of people are going that way. But the road to eternal life is narrow and the gate is small, and few people look hard enough to find it.

"Watch out for false prophets who disguise themselves as harmless sheep. Inwardly they are like wolves ready to tear you apart. Before you believe what they say, wait and see what fruit they produce. Do people go to thornbushes for grapes, or to tall thistles for figs? A good tree will produce good fruit, and a bad tree, bad fruit. A good tree will not produce bad fruit, nor will a bad tree produce good fruit. Every tree that does not produce good fruit will be cut down and thrown into the fire. The way to know where people stand is by the fruit they produce.

"Not everyone who calls Me 'Lord' will enter the kingdom of heaven—only those who obey My Father in heaven. When the day of judgment comes, they will say, 'Lord, did we not preach in Your name, and in Your name perform miracles and cast out demons?' I will have to tell them, 'I don't recognize you. Go away. You did all this for your own glory.'

"Those who listen to what I say and obey are like the man who built his house on solid rock. When the rains and floods came and strong winds beat against the house, it stood because it was built on solid rock. But those who don't take to heart what I say and don't obey are like the man who built his house on sand. When the rains and floods came and strong winds beat against the house, it shifted, broke apart, and was washed away."

When Jesus finished, the people were amazed because He spoke with authority and made things so easy to understand, not like the scribes and Pharisees (Matt. 6:1-7:29).

seven

Jesus Responds to People's Needs

When Jesus had finished teaching from the hillside, He decided to go back to Capernaum. A Roman captain lived there, whose servant was terribly sick and about to die. His servant was like one of the officer's family, and he loved him very much. So when the captain heard about Jesus' power to heal, he asked the Jewish leaders in his community to urge Jesus to come and heal his servant. They went and pleaded with Jesus, "Please come and heal this man's servant! He deserves it because he loves our people and has even built a synagogue for us."

So Jesus went with them. He was not far from the officer's house when the captain sent a couple of his friends to say to Jesus, "Lord, I don't deserve to have You come to my house. The reason I didn't personally go to see You is that I'm not worthy even to talk to You. I know that all You have to do is to give the word and my servant will be healed. I know about the power of authority, because I have to obey those over me, and my soldiers have to obey me. I say to this one, 'Go,' and he goes, and to that one, 'Come,' and he comes. I tell my servant to do this, and he does it."

When Jesus heard this, He was surprised at the Roman military man's faith. Turning to the crowd, He said, "I tell you, I have not seen such faith in Me among My own people." Jesus gave the word, and when the captain's friends returned to the house, they found the servant healed (Luke 7:1–10).

As Jesus continued on His way, two blind men followed Him, shouting, "Son of David, have mercy on us!" When Jesus went into the house where He was staying, they followed Him inside.

Jesus asked, "Do you really believe that I can heal you?"

They answered, "Yes, Lord."

Jesus touched their eyes and said, "Because of your faith, so be it." Instantly the men could see. Then He warned them, "Don't tell people who healed you."

As Jesus left the house, someone brought to Him a demon-possessed man who could not talk. Jesus cast out the demon, and the man could speak again. People were amazed and said, "Nothing like this has ever happened in Israel before!"

But the Pharisees said, "He didn't heal the man by the power of God, but by the power of the ruler of demons" (Matt. 9:27-34).

Jesus said nothing but continued on His way, going from village to village sharing the good news of God's kingdom. Not only did the disciples accompany Him, but also some women whom Jesus had healed of various diseases and freed from devil possession. One was Mary Magdelene, out of whom He had cast seven devils; Joanna, the wife of the manager of Herod's palace; Susanna; and others who used their means to help support Jesus and His disciples (Luke 8:1-3).

One day Jesus decided to go with His disciples to the village of Nain, and as usual a large crowd of people followed Him. As He neared the village, a funeral procession came out carrying the body of a young man, a widow's only son, followed by a number of mourners. When Jesus saw the mother weeping, His heart went out to her and He told her not to cry. Then He stopped the procession, went up to the body, and said, "Young man, get up!" The dead man opened his eyes, sat up, and began to talk. Then Jesus told him to stand up, and when he did, Jesus gave him back to his mother.

For a moment the people were stunned. Then they praised God and said, "A great prophet has come! God has sent him to help His people!" The news of what happened spread throughout Judah and even across the border to neighboring countries (Luke 7:11-17).

Accused of Witchcraft

Jesus went into the village and healed all the sick who came to Him. Then people brought a demon-possessed man who was both blind and could not talk. Jesus cast out the demon and healed the man so that he could see and talk.

Amazed, the people said to each other, "Could this be the Messiah, the Son of David?"

But the Pharisees once again said, "He is doing this by the power of the ruler of the demons. How else could He do it?"

Jesus knew what they were thinking and said to them, "Any kingdom at war with itself can't survive. It's the same for a city or a family. If they fight each other, their union won't last. And if Satan is using his power to cast out his fellow demons, he's fighting against himself. How can his kingdom last?

"If I cast out demons by the ruler of demons, what power did the prophets from your people use to cast them out? But if I'm casting out demons by the power of the Spirit, then you're seeing the kingdom of God at work right in front of you. How can anyone enter a strong man's house to rob him unless he first overcomes the man and ties him up? Then he can take what he wants. If you're not *for* Me, you're *against* Me. There's no neutral ground.

"Let Me tell you, every sin can be forgiven, even blasphemy, but what cannot be forgiven is rejecting the work and power of the Spirit. Anyone who falsely accuses Me can be forgiven, but anyone who turns against the Holy Spirit cannot be forgiven, either in this world or at the ushering in of the world to come.

"A tree is known by its fruit. A good tree will produce good fruit, and a bad tree, bad fruit. Your thoughts are like the fangs of a poisonous snake. How can evil-thinking men judge what is good and right? Whatever is in a man's heart, that's what comes out. A good man says good things, and an evil-thinking man says bad things. In the judgment all will have to face what they did and said. The way people think and talk will determine their future—they will be either forgiven or condemned" (Matt. 12:22-37).

Then the Pharisees said, "Show us an unquestionable miracle as a sign to show us that You are from God."

Jesus replied, "Only a faithless and evil generation would ask for a sign like that. The only miracle beyond question is the sign of Jonah, which I will give you in due time. Just as Jonah was in the belly of the great fish for three days and nights and came out alive, so the Son of Man will be in the heart of the earth for three days and nights. The people of Nineveh listened to Jonah and repented. The judgment will condemn this generation for its blindness because someone greater than Jonah is here, and yet you refuse to repent and change your ways.

"In the judgment the queen of Sheba also will condemn you, for she came to Jerusalem to listen to Solomon. Someone greater than Solomon is here, yet you refuse to listen to Him.

"When an evil spirit is cast out of a man, it is very restless. Not finding peace, it says, 'I will go back to the man I came from.' When it returns, it finds its former home empty, swept, and clean. Then it goes and invites seven other spirits more evil than itself to come also and move into the man, and they do. Now the man is worse off than he was before. This will be the experience of this wicked, faithless generation who keep Me out of their hearts."

Jesus' Family

Then Jesus turned from the Pharisees and began teaching the people.

Later His mother and stepbrothers arrived at the house that Jesus had been invited to and stood outside, trying to get in to talk to Him.

Someone said to Jesus, "Your mother and brothers are outside asking for You." Jesus asked, "Who is My mother? Who are My brothers?" He turned to the people and said, "These are My mother and brothers. Anyone who does the will of My Father is My brother, sister, and mother."

Jesus went outside to talk to His family. Then He went down to the lake, and the people followed Him. There was such a large crowd that He got into a boat, sat down, and taught the people on the shore by using stories.

Stories

"Listen!" Jesus said. "A farmer went out to sow. As he flung his seeds across the field, some fell on the nearby footpath, and the birds quickly came and ate them. Some fell on rocky places with little soil. The seeds quickly sprouted, but under the heat of the sun they soon wilted and died because their roots were not very deep. Some fell among thorns and weeds, which grew faster and choked the sprouting seeds. Still others fell on good soil and produced 30, 60, or 100 times as much as was sown. He who has ears to hear should listen and think about what I've said."

Later Jesus' disciples asked Him, "Why do You always use stories when You teach the people?"

Jesus replied, "Your hearts are already open to the things of the kingdom of heaven, but the hearts of others are closed. To those who listen with their hearts to what I'm saying, more understanding of the kingdom will be given. But to those who are listening only with their ears, even what they hear will be lost. I use stories to knock on the doors of people's hearts. But some keep their hearts closed. So they hear what I am saying but don't understand. They keep looking, but they don't see.

"This is what Isaiah meant when he said, 'You hear but never understand. You see, yet you're blind. You have hardened your hearts, shut your eyes, and closed your ears. You don't turn to God to let Him heal you.' How blessed you are! You have eyes that see and ears that hear. Many prophets and godly men have longed to hear and see what you see and hear, but never had the chance.

"Here's what the story of the farmer means: The seed is the Word of God, and the sower is the Son of God. The footpath represents those who hear what I'm saying but don't open their hearts. Then the evil one quickly comes and takes away what they've heard. The rocky places with shallow soil represent those who receive the Word of God with joy, but the Word never takes root. When troubles come and living a godly life becomes hard, they quickly give up. The soil with thorns and weeds represents those who hear the Word, and it takes root and sprouts; but it can't grow as it should. The cares of this life and the deceptiveness of money choke the Word, and it never grows big enough to bear fruit. The good soil represents those who hear the Word, take it to heart, and produce a 30-, 60-, or 100-fold harvest."

Then Jesus illustrated with another story: "The kingdom of heaven is like a farmer who sowed good seed in his field. But that night, while everyone was asleep, his enemy came and sowed weeds in the field. When the wheat came up, so did the weeds.

"The farm workers came to the owner and said, 'Sir, you gave us good seed to sow in the field, which we did. Where did the weeds come from?'

"He answered, 'My enemy did this.'

"They asked, 'Do you want us to go and pull up the weeds before they get bigger?'

"He replied, 'No, because as you pull up the weeds, you will pull up some of the wheat also. Let them grow together until the harvest; then I'll tell the harvesters to sort things out. They'll tie the weeds in bundles and burn them up and will bring the wheat into my barn.' "

Jesus then used another story: "The beginning of the kingdom of heaven is like a tiny seed of a mustard plant that a man planted in his garden. Even though it's the smallest of all seeds, when it sprouts and grows it becomes the biggest plant in the garden—a small tree—and the birds come and build their nests there.

"The growth of God's kingdom is like the quiet action of yeast that a woman mixes into her bread dough; then silently the dough begins to rise."

Jesus used many more such stories to help the people understand the kingdom of God. He fulfilled the prophecy about the Messiah that said, "I will open my mouth and tell you stories. I will use illustrations from everyday life to teach people things not understood since the creation of the world."

Jesus had the disciples row back to shore, and when He got out, someone invited Him to his house. He accepted and, once they were seated, His disciples asked Him to explain the meaning of the weeds sown in the field. He said, "I am the farmer who plants good seeds. The field is the world. The good seed represents good people who love and serve God. The weeds represent wicked people. The enemy who sowed them is the devil. The harvest is the end of the world, and the harvesters are the angels.

"Just as the weeds are separated from the wheat at harvesttime and burned up, so will it be at the end of the world. I will come back with My angels and remove everything that causes sin and all those who do evil.

Like the weeds of the field, the wicked will be consumed. They will suffer bitter remorse, but the godly will be happy and will shine like the sun in the kingdom of their heavenly Father. Those who have ears to hear should listen to what I'm saying and take it to heart.

"The kingdom of heaven is like treasure buried in a field. When a man finds it, he covers it up and quickly sells everything he has to buy the field. The kingdom of heaven is like a merchant on the lookout for precious pearls. When he finds one of extreme value, he sells everything he has and buys it.

"The kingdom of heaven can be compared to a fishing net that is thrown out into the water and catches all kinds of fish. When it's full, they pull it back to shore and sit down to sort out the fish. They put the good fish into baskets and throw the bad ones away. That's how it will be at the end of the world. The angels will sort the good from the bad, keeping the good and leaving the bad ones for the fire. There will be lots of weeping and some very painful regrets. Do you understand?"

The disciples answered, "Yes, we do."

Jesus responded, "Every disciple who understands what the kingdom of heaven is all about is like the owner of a store who goes to the storeroom and brings out treasures new and old to offer the people what they need."

Then Jesus got up, thanked His host, and continued on His way (Matt. 12:38–13:53).

eight

Difficult Days

As Jesus and His disciples were walking along, a young religious teacher came to Him and said, "Master, let me be one of Your disciples. I'll follow You wherever You go."

Jesus answered, "Foxes have dens and birds have nests, but I have no place to call My own."

Then another young man spoke up: "Lord, my father just died, and I need to go and help make funeral arrangements and bury him. Then I'll come and follow You."

Jesus replied, "Others can make the arrangements. You need to decide first if you want to be My disciple" (Matt. 8:19-22).

Wherever Jesus went, large crowds followed Him. When He got to the lake, He said to His disciples, "Let's get in the boat and cross to the other side to get away from the crowds and get some rest." So they did, but other boats followed. Halfway across, a powerful storm suddenly swept across the lake, and waves began washing over the sides of the boat, filling it with water.

Jesus, totally exhausted, was in the back of the boat sleeping. The storm became so violent that the disciples finally shook Jesus awake, shouting, "Lord, save us, or we'll all drown!"

Jesus stood up, rebuked the wind, and said to the waves, "Be still!"

Instantly the wind stopped and the lake became calm. Then He turned to His disciples and said, "Why were you so afraid? Where is your faith?"

They were filled with awe and said to each other, "What kind of man is this who speaks to the wind and the waves, and they obey Him?" (Matt. 8:18, 23-27).

When they arrived at the other side of the lake, in the area of the people called Gadarenes, two demon-possessed men living among the rocks and tombs came running down the hill toward them. These men were so violent that after they had been bound and taken away, they broke their chains and were driven by the demons back into the wilderness. Always screaming and cutting themselves, they terrorized that whole region. They headed straight for Jesus. When they got near Him, they fell on their knees, shouting, "You are the Son of God! Leave us alone! Have You come to destroy us ahead of time?"

Jesus asked the demons, "What is your name?" They answered, "Our name is Legion, for we are many."

Not far distant was a large herd of pigs. The demons asked Jesus, "If You have to cast us out of these men, let us go into that herd of pigs."

Jesus said, "Go!"

So the demons left the two men and took control of the pigs. Suddenly the herd of about 2,000 pigs went wild. They ran down the hill, plunged into the lake, and drowned. The herdsmen ran back to town and told the farmers and everyone they met what had happened to the pigs and the demon-possessed men. The pig farmers and the people wanted to see for themselves. When they saw that the pigs were gone and the two men were sitting at the feet of Jesus, dressed and in their right minds, they were afraid. Then the pig farmers, as well as the people, asked Jesus to leave and never come back.

So Jesus and His disciples went back to the boat to return to Capernaum. The two men begged to go along. But Jesus wouldn't let them. He said, "Go home and tell your family and friends what the Lord has done for you and how merciful He has been."

The two men left and told their story all over town and throughout the province of Decapolis about what Jesus had done for them. And the people were amazed (Matt. 8:28-34; Mark 5:1-20; Luke 8:26-39).

A Little Girl

As soon as Jesus reached the other side of the lake, people came from everywhere to see Him. A leader of the local synagogue named Jairus fell on his knees in front of Jesus and pleaded with Him, "My little daughter is about to die. Please come and put Your hands on her so she will get well and live." Jesus went with him, and the people followed.

A woman who had been menstruating continuously for 12 years was in the crowd. She had gone to numerous doctors and had spent all she had, but was no better. In fact, she was getting worse. When she heard about Jesus, she decided to go and see Him. She pressed through the crowd and came up behind Him, saying to herself, "If I can only touch His robe, I know I'll be healed." As she did so, suddenly the bleeding stopped and she knew that she was well!

At that moment Jesus felt power go out from Him. He turned around and asked, "Who touched My robe?"

The disciples said, "With all the people crowding around You, pushing and shoving, how can You ask, 'Who touched My robe?'"

But Jesus kept looking around at the crowd to see who had done it. Then the woman came forward and, trembling with fear, fell on her knees and told Him that she was the one. Jesus quietly said, "Daughter, don't be afraid. Your faith in Me has made you well. Go in peace."

While Jesus was speaking to the woman, Jairus' servants came and said to him, "Don't bother the Rabbi. Your daughter is dead."

Jesus overheard what they told Jairus, so He turned to him and said, "Don't be sad. Trust Me."

Then He told the crowd not to follow Him to Jairus' house, but He did take Peter, James, and John with Him. When they got there, the town's mourners had already come. Jesus went inside and said to them, "Why are you wailing so? The girl isn't dead. She's sleeping."

They laughed at Him. He insisted that they wait outside. Then after escorting the father, mother, and the three disciples into the room where the little girl was, He took her by the hand and said to her, "Little girl, it's time to wake up."

The little girl opened her eyes and got up. She looked around and ran to her parents, who stood there stunned. They couldn't believe that their 12-year-old daughter was alive. Jesus said to her parents, "Give her something to eat. And don't tell people what I did" (Mark 5:21-43; Luke 8:56).

John in Prison

When John, who was in prison, heard what Jesus was doing, he sent word to two of his disciples to ask Jesus, "Are You the one who is to come to save Israel, or should the people look for someone else?" When John's disciples found Jesus, they said, "John sent us to ask whether you are the one to save Israel, or whether the Deliverer is still to come."

Jesus said nothing, but continued to teach the people and heal them of all sorts of diseases, demon possession, and blindness. This went on all day. Late in the afternoon Jesus turned to John's two disciples and said, "Go tell John what you've seen and heard. Tell him that the blind see, the disabled walk, the lepers are healed, the deaf hear, the dead have been raised, and the good news about God is spreading everywhere. Blessed is the man whose doubts disappear when he thinks of Me" (Luke 7:18-23).

The two disciples went back to John and told him what they had seen Jesus do and what He had said to them.

As soon as they had gone, Jesus turned to the people and asked, "When you went to the river Jordan, where John was preaching, what did you go out to see? A reed blowing in the wind? A man dressed in the latest fashion? Those who are well dressed live in beautiful houses. So what did you go out to see? A prophet? Yes, a prophet, but even more than a prophet. The Scripture talks about this in Malachi when God says, 'I will send My messenger ahead of the Messiah to prepare the way for Him.' I want to tell you that no prophet is greater than John. Yet those who see what I do and hear what I say are more privileged than John.

"Beginning with John's ministry, the good news of the kingdom has brought opposition, but the kingdom is advancing, and the courageous urge others to take hold of it. What Moses and all the prophets wrote about the Messiah points to this time. John is another Elijah, the prophet that everyone expects to come before the Messiah does. Those of you who have ears to hear, listen to what I'm saying.

"To what should I compare the people of this generation? They are like children playing games in the public square. One group says to the other, 'When we played wedding songs on our flutes, you didn't want to dance or sing. Then we decided to play funeral songs, but you didn't want to mourn and cry.' That's how people relate to John and Me. John lived a very strict life, not eating and drinking with others, and some said, 'He's fanatical.' Then I came along and ate with tax collectors and sinners, and they said, 'He's no better than a drunkard and a glutton.'"

Jesus expressed His disappointment in the people who lived in the cities in which He had performed His greatest miracles, because they hadn't turned to God or changed their ways. "Woe to you, Korazin and Bethsaida! If the miracles I did in you had been done in the foreign cities of Tyre and Sidon, their people would have repented with ashes on their heads. Those people will fare better in the judgment than you. And you, Capernaum, do you think you're better than other cities? Not so. Because of your pride, you will be brought down and destroyed. If the miracles I performed in you had been done in Sodom, it would still be there today. Sodom will fare better in the judgment than you."

Then Jesus looked up and prayed, "I praise You, Father, Lord of heaven and earth. Thank You for revealing Yourself to people of child-like faith, and keeping Yourself from those who think they are so wise and learned. Yes, Father, that's the way You have always worked."

Turning back to the people, Jesus said, "My Father has given Me authority over everything because He knows Me as no one else does. And no one knows the Father as I do. I'm sharing the Father with you. Come to Me, you who are weary and burdened, and I will give you rest. Yoke up with Me and learn from Me. I am humble and gentle, and you will find rest in Me. My teachings are easy, and My burdens are light" (Matt. 11:7–30).

nine

Jesus Expands His Ministry

Jesus left Capernaum and, with His disciples, went to visit His hometown of Nazareth again. On Sabbath He went to the synagogue, and when the people saw Him, they wanted Him to speak. He agreed, and as they listened, they were amazed at His teaching. They asked each other, "Where did He learn all this? Where did He get such insight into Scripture? Where does He get the power to perform the miracles He does? He's just a carpenter, the son of Mary and the stepbrother of James, Joseph, Jude, and Simon. And His stepsisters, too, live right here in town." But even as they listened, they hardened their hearts and refused to accept His teachings. "Who does He think He is," they asked, "telling us how to live?" They became deeply offended and refused to believe in Him.

Then Jesus said to them, "A prophet is respected and listened to everywhere except in his own hometown among those he grew up with." Because of their unbelief, He worked no great miracles in Nazareth, except to heal a few people who had faith in Him. He was greatly disappointed at the unbelief of the people. So He left and went to preach and teach in other cities and towns (Mark 6:1-6).

Wherever He went, He healed people of all kinds of sicknesses and diseases. His heart filled with compassion as He saw crowds of needy people coming to Him for help. They seemed so fragile, like sheep without a shepherd. Jesus turned to His disciples and said, "The harvest is very great, but the laborers are so few. Pray that the Lord will send more workers into the field."

Jesus Asks the Twelve to Help

One day Jesus called His disciples together and gave them power to help Him cast out demons and heal the sick. He said to them, "Go to the people of Israel. Tell them that the kingdom of God is here. Then give them a glimpse of the kingdom by healing the sick, cleansing the lepers, raising the dead, and casting out demons. Do this graciously and free of charge. Freely you have received, freely give.

"Don't carry any gold or silver in your belts, no beggar's bag, extra clothes, sandals, or even a walking stick, because the people will give you what you need. When you come to a city or village, ask for a man who is respected and hospitable and stay with him until you leave for the next town. If a family invites you to stay with them, be grateful and bless that family. If they're good people, the blessing will stand. But if they try to take advantage of your healing powers, thank them for their hospitality and leave, and the blessing will be removed. If a city or village doesn't welcome you or listen to what you have to say, leave and shake the dust off your feet. I assure you that the record of Sodom and Gomorrah will look better in the judgment than the cities and towns that reject you.

"Your work won't be easy, because I'm sending you as sheep among wolves. You will need to be as wise as serpents and as harmless as doves. Be aware of people, because some will report you to the local leaders, who will have you arrested and whipped right in their own synagogues. You will be brought before governors and kings because of me. This will give you a chance to tell them who I am. When this happens, don't worry about what to say or how to say it. The Holy Spirit will give you the right words to say and will help you say them in the right spirit. The Father Himself will speak through you.

"The time is coming when brother will betray brother, fathers will betray their children, and children will turn against their parents and have them put to death. People will hate you because of Me. But those who stand firm will have a place with Me in My kingdom. When they persecute you in one place, go to another. But you will not be able to go to every city and town in Israel before I complete My mission.

"A student is not greater than his teacher. A servant is not greater than his master. The student identifies with his teacher, and the servant with his master. So if they say that I, your master and teacher, have a demon, how much more will they say that about you! But don't be afraid. The time is coming when everything that was said secretly will be made public. What I've told you at night, preach boldly during the day. What I've whispered in your ear, shout from the rooftops for all to hear.

"Don't be afraid of those who want to kill you. They can kill only your body—they cannot touch your soul. God is the only one who can destroy both your body and soul. But He loves you. Not even a sparrow falls to the ground without your Father's noticing it. He even knows the number of hairs on your head. So don't be afraid. You're worth much more to Him than a sky full of sparrows.

"Anyone who is not ashamed to stand up for Me publicly, I will not be ashamed to stand up for him before all of heaven and introduce him to the Father. But if anyone denies knowing Me, I will not admit knowing him before heaven or before the Father.

"Don't think that My coming here will bring global peace. My coming is like a two-edged sword. It brings the good news of salvation, but it can also bring persecution. It can turn a son against his father, a daughter against her mother, and in-laws against each other. Your enemies could come from your own family. If you think more highly of your father or mother or son or daughter than of Me, then you're not worthy of being My disciple. If you cling to your life more than to Me, you will lose it, but if you're willing to give up your life for Me, you'll get it back again.

"Anyone who welcomes you is welcoming Me, and anyone who welcomes Me is welcoming the Father who sent Me. Those who love Me will love you, too. Anyone who receives you as he would an inspired prophet will receive a prophet's reward, and anyone who receives you as he would a godly man will receive a godly man's reward. Anyone who gives a cup of cold water to one of the least of My followers will be rewarded."

After Jesus finished telling these things to His disciples, He went on to preach, teach, and heal people. And so did His disciples (Matt. 9:35-11:1).

John's Execution

When Herod, who ruled Galilee, heard about Jesus and how popular He was, he said to himself, "This must be John the Baptist risen from the dead. That's why He can do such miracles." Others said, "He must be Elijah come back from heaven." Still others said, "This must be the prophet Moses talked about coming, or one of the other great prophets." But Herod Antipas insisted, "This is John the Baptist, whom I beheaded. He's come back from the dead!"

Herod said this because he had arrested John and put him in prison for the sake of Herodias, his wife, who had been the wife of his half brother Philip. She had left Philip to marry Herod. John had told Herod that it was not right for him to marry his brother's wife. That's why Herodias wanted John killed, but she couldn't do anything about it, because Herod believed that John was a holy man and he protected him. Though Herod was perplexed whenever he talked to John, he liked to listen to him.

Herodias' chance to get rid of John finally came. It happened at Herod's birthday party when the banquet hall was filled with high officials, army officers, and dignitaries from all over Galilee. At the height of the party Herodias sent her daughter to go in and dance for the guests. Herod, in high spirits, was so pleased that he said to the girl, "Ask for anything you want, and I'll give it to you." Then, wanting to impress the guests, he rashly took an oath and added, "I'll even give you up to half of my kingdom!"

She thanked him and went to her mother and said, "What should I ask for?"

Without hesitation her mother replied, "Ask for the head of John the Baptist."

So the girl hurried back and said to the king, "I would like the head of John the Baptist on a platter."

The king was shocked, and so was everyone else. He was terribly sorry for what he had promised, but dared not break his oath in front of his guests. So he sent for the executioner and ordered him to cut off John's head and bring it to him on a platter. The executioner went to the prison, beheaded John, and brought his head to the king on a platter as ordered. Herod told him to give it to the girl, who took it and gave it to her mother.

When John's disciples heard about it, they went to the prison to get his body and then buried it in a tomb (Mark 6:14-29).

Jesus was so saddened by the news that He wanted to be alone. So He got into a boat and asked His disciples to row across the lake to a deserted place where they could talk to Him about their recent mission trip and rest awhile. This was about the time of the Jewish Passover, when people were making their way to Jerusalem (Matt. 14:13; Mark 6:30-32; John 6:4).

ten

Jesus Feeds People

People saw Jesus and His disciples leave and decided to follow, some in boats and others by foot around the lake. They kept looking for Jesus until they found Him. People were constantly streaming in to talk to Jesus and His disciples, so they didn't even have time to eat.

When Jesus saw all those people and realized how far they had come, His heart went out to them. They looked like sheep without a shepherd. So He asked them to sit down, and He began teaching them.

Late in the afternoon His disciples said to Him, "This is an out-of-the-way place and a long way from any town. It's late in the afternoon, and soon the sun will set. Don't You think we ought to send the people home so that they can get to some nearby villages to buy something to eat before it gets dark?"

Jesus said to Philip, "Maybe we should go to buy some bread for these people?" He said this to test his faith.

Philip replied, "How can we buy enough bread to feed all these people? That would cost hundreds of days' wages!"

Andrew said, "There's a young boy here who has five round flatbreads and two small fish. But what good is that for all these people?"

Then Jesus told the disciples to have the people sit down in groups of 50 wherever they could find some grass.

After they were seated, Jesus took the bread and fish, looked up to heaven, gave thanks, and blessed the food. He broke the bread into pieces and handed some bread and fish to each disciple to give to the people. Everyone in the crowd ate until they were full. There was even food left over. About 5,000, not counting women and children, were fed that day.

After everyone had eaten, Jesus said to His disciples, "Pick up what's left so that nothing is wasted." They went among the people and collected 12 basketfuls of leftovers.

The men in the crowd said, "This is the Prophet that Moses told us would come to be among us!"

Jesus quickly sensed that they were ready to take Him by force to make Him king of Israel. So He told the disciples to get back into their boat and cross to the other side of the lake and He would meet them there. Then He dismissed the people with such authority that no one dared disobey (Matt. 14:13-22; Mark 6:30-45; Luke 9:10-17; John 6:1-17).

Jesus Walks on Water

When everyone had gone, Jesus climbed a nearby hill overlooking the lake, to be alone and pray. He watched the disciples get into the boat and begin rowing across the lake. When they were about halfway across the lake a storm hit, blowing them off course. Soon waves were washing over the side of the boat.

Sometime after midnight the disciples were so tired from rowing that they finally gave up and just let the boat toss with the waves. Jesus decided to help them. He made His way down the hill to the lake and began walking across the water toward the boat. When the disciples saw Him, they thought He was a ghost and cried out to God for help. Jesus responded, "Don't be afraid! It's Me—Jesus!"

Then Peter called out, "Lord! If that's really You, let me walk on the water and come to You."

Jesus called back, "Come!"

So Peter jumped over the side of the boat and began walking on the water toward Jesus. But when he took his eyes off of Jesus and looked at the high waves, he became frightened and started to sink. He cried out, "Lord! Save me!"

Jesus grabbed Peter's outstretched hand, pulled him up, and said, "Why did you take your eyes off me and begin to doubt?" Jesus and Peter walked to the boat together, and as soon as they got in, the wind stopped. Then all the disciples worshipped Him, saying, "Lord, You really are the Son of God!" (Matt. 14:23-33).

The next thing they knew, they were on the other side of the lake—near Capernaum (John 6:21).

After they had tied up the boat and gotten out, the people recognized them and ran home to bring their sick to be healed. Word spread, and soon people were bringing their sick relatives and friends from all directions. They begged Him just to let them touch His robe, and as they did, they were healed (Matt. 14:34-36).

Jesus Misunderstood

In the meanwhile, back across the lake, some of the people who had been with Jesus the previous afternoon had stayed overnight. In the morning they expected to see Him coming down from the hill because His disciples had left without Him. When they couldn't find Him, they wondered where He had gone. Then some boats from Tiberias landed nearby on their way to Capernaum. The people got in and went across the lake looking for Him. When they found Him, they said, "Teacher, how did You get here?"

Jesus answered, "The reason you looked so hard to find Me is that you saw Me work a miracle to feed you. Don't think only about food, but about things that will last and give you eternal life, which only the Son of Man can give you. For this I have the Father's approval."

They asked, "What do we have to do to receive God's approval?"

Jesus answered, "The first thing is to believe in the one whom He has sent."

They said, "You need to give us a sign so that we can believe that You're the one whom God has sent. Our ancestors had the miracle of manna while in the wilderness as a sign that God had sent Moses. You know the Scripture says, 'Moses gave them bread from heaven so they wouldn't go hungry.'"

Jesus replied, "Moses wasn't the one who gave your ancestors bread from heaven. God was. Now God's eternal manna has come down from heaven to give life to the world."

They responded, "Lord, this is the kind of bread we need! Give it to us, and we'll eat it."

Jesus said, "I am God's bread from heaven. No one who comes to Me will go spiritually hungry again, nor will they go thirsty. Yesterday you saw Me perform a miracle, which should have been enough of a sign, yet you still don't believe in Me. Anyone whom the Father sends to Me I will not turn away, but I will feed them because they believe in Me. I have come to do, not My own will, but the will of Him who sent Me. My Father's will is that I not lose one of those He sends to me, but in the last days I will raise them from the dead and give them eternal life. The Father wants everyone to be saved. I assure you that when the end comes, I will resurrect all those who believe in Me."

Then the religious leaders and others in the crowd expressed their doubts about Jesus because He had said, "I am the bread from heaven." They said to each other, "Isn't He the son of Joseph? We know His parents, His family. How can He say, 'I have come down from heaven'?"

Jesus answered, "Don't doubt what I said about Myself. No one can come to Me unless He responds to the Father, who will draw him to Me, and in the end I will raise him from the dead. As the Scripture says: 'They will all be taught by the Lord.' So everyone who listens to the Father will come to Me. Not that they have seen the Father, but I have seen Him and have been sent by Him. Let Me assure you, everyone who believes in Me has already tasted eternal life. I am the bread of life. Your ancestors ate manna in the wilderness, but died. Those who eat the spiritual bread from heaven will not die. I am that spiritual bread. Anyone who eats this bread will live forever. This bread is my body, which I will give for the world so that people may live."

The religious leaders and the people began arguing among themselves, saying, "How can He feed the whole world, and who would want to eat His body?"

Jesus answered, "I'm telling you, unless you eat the body of the Son of Man and drink His blood, you cannot have eternal life. But those who eat and drink from Me have already found eternal life, and in the last days I will raise them from the dead. My body is food, and My blood is drink. Those who continue to eat and drink from Me will live in Me, and I in them. Just as I feed on the love of the Father who sent Me, so those who feed on My love will live because of Me. I am the true bread from heaven. Anyone who eats this spiritual bread will not die as your ancestors did, but will live forever." These are the things that Jesus taught in the synagogue in Capernaum.

After He had said this, many of Jesus' followers and even His disciples said to each other, "This is too hard to understand. It just doesn't make sense. Who can believe all that?" Jesus knew that they were talking about Him, so He said to them, "Are you offended by what I said? What would you say if you saw the Son of Man go back to heaven again? It is the Holy Spirit who gives life. Human effort can't produce it. The words that I speak are spirit and life. But some of you don't believe Me." Jesus already knew who didn't believe and who would betray Him. So He continued, "That's why I told you that people can't come to Me unless they first respond to the drawing power of the Father."

At this point many of His followers turned away from Him. Then Jesus asked His disciples, "Are you going to leave Me too?"

Peter answered, "Lord, to whom can we go? You are the only one who has the words of eternal life. We believe what You say. We know that You are the Christ, the Son of the living God."

Jesus responded, "Didn't I call each of you to come and follow Me and be My disciple? Yet one of you came of his own accord, and the devil has made him his ally." He was talking about Judas, who would later betray him.

Soon it would be time for the Feast of Tabernacles, but Jesus decided not to go to Jerusalem, because the Jewish leaders were looking for an excuse to kill Him. So He continued His ministry in Galilee (John 6:22-7:2).

Jesus Corrects the Pharisees

One day some Pharisees and teachers of the law from Jerusalem went to Galilee to confront Jesus. When they noticed that some of His disciples didn't follow the Jewish ritual of washing their hands a certain way, they criticized them. Jews, especially the Pharisees, washed their hands meticulously before they ate, and doubly so after they came back from the market. They also clung to such traditions as washing cups, pitchers, and kettles in specific ways.

After the Pharisees and the teachers of the law had criticized the disciples, they turned to Jesus and sarcastically asked, "Why don't Your disciples follow our ancient tradition of washing their hands this same way before they eat?"

Jesus answered, "Isaiah was right when he spoke for God, saying, 'These people honor Me with their lips, but don't love Me with their hearts. They worship Me, but they put their own traditions above My commandments.' You're doing the same thing. You pay more attention to keeping your hands clean than to keeping God's commandments. Let Me give you another example; Moses said, 'Honor your father and mother. Anyone who turns away from his parents and curses them should be put to death.' But you tell the people that it's all right to say to your parents, 'Sorry, I can't help you. I've promised to give all my money to the Temple when I die.' You let people turn away from their needy parents and break the commandment just so you can get their money. You put your own rules above the law of God. I could give you many more examples of how hypocritical you are."

Then Jesus addressed the people: "Listen to Me and try to understand what I'm saying. You don't become impure if you eat without washing your hands. It's not what goes into your mouth that defiles you, but what comes out of it. Think about what I've just said."

Afterward Jesus accepted an invitation to someone's house to get away from the crowds. When they got there, His disciples asked Him to explain what He meant by not becoming impure. Jesus said, "You mean that you don't understand either? Can't you see that whatever goes into your mouth from unwashed hands won't defile you? It only goes into your stomach and out again. But what is hidden in your heart and comes out of your mouth is what really matters. It's in the heart that impurity begins and produces wicked thoughts, immorality, theft, murder, adultery, greed, wickedness, jealousy, deception, hostility, suspicion, slander, pride, arrogance, and all kinds of foolish desires. These things come from the inside and are what make your behavior unacceptable to God" (Mark 7:1-23).

eleven

Jesus Selects His Places of Ministry

Then Jesus left Galilee and crossed the border into the province of Syria. From there He headed north toward the cities of Tyre and Sidon. He tried to travel quietly, but before long, news that He was in the area spread, and people came from everywhere to see Him.

One day a Canaanite woman fell at the feet of Jesus and tearfully pleaded, "Have mercy on me, Son of David! My daughter is possessed by a demon. Please heal her!"

But contrary to His usual compassion, Jesus ignored her, as any pious Jew would. His disciples urged Him to send her away. To demonstrate to His disciples the harshness of prejudiced thinking, Jesus continued in the same vein.

He said to the woman, "I was sent to help My own people in Israel."

Again she begged him, "Lord, please help me!"

Jesus spoke kindly but firmly, "It's not right to take food away from the children to feed the dogs."

She replied, "Sir, that's true, but even family dogs are given crumbs from what's left of the children's food."

Jesus smiled and said, "Woman, what faith you have! You have answered well. Your daughter is now healed." When the woman got home, she found her daughter quietly resting in bed, demon-free (Matt. 15:21–28; Mark 7:24–30).

Then Jesus left the area of Tyre and Sidon and returned to Galilee. From there He went on to the region of the Decapolis, east of the lake. While He was there, the people brought to Him a deaf man who could hardly talk. They begged Jesus to heal him. So He took him aside, put his fingers in the man's ears, took some moisture from his own lips, and touched the tip of the man's tongue. Then He looked up to heaven, gave a big sigh, and said, "Open up!" Instantly the man could both hear and speak!

Jesus told the people not to spread the news of what He had done. But the more He told them why they shouldn't do it, the more they shouted His praise and spread the news everywhere. They said to everyone they met, "This man Jesus does amazing things, and He does them well. He not only made a deaf man hear, but also made him speak again!" (Mark 7:31-37).

Jesus Feeds Additional Thousands

After this experience, Jesus made his way to a secluded spot near the lake and climbed a hill to rest a while. Soon people brought him the lame, blind, mute, crippled, and many others with physical problems. And He healed all of them. The people were amazed when they heard the mute speak, the blind see, and the lame walk. As they watched, they began praising the God of Israel.

After all the sick were healed Jesus said to His disciples, "I feel sorry for the people. We've been here for three days, and all this time they haven't had much to eat. If we send them away without feeding them, some will faint before they get home, because they've come a long way."

His disciples replied, "Where are we supposed to get enough food to feed all these people?"

Jesus answered, "Don't we have something to share with them?"

They said, "All we have is seven round flatbreads and a few small fish."

Jesus turned to the people and asked them to sit down. Then, taking the bread and the fish, He thanked God for what He had. Then He broke the bread and gave each disciple a piece, along with a small fish, and told them to share it with the people.

The people ate until they were full, and the disciples picked up seven large basketfuls of leftovers. The number of people Jesus fed that day was 4,000 men, not counting women and children. Then Jesus dismissed the people and sent them home. As they were leaving, He went down to the lake, got into the fishing boat, and headed south along the coast to the area near Magadan (Matt. 15:29-39).

When the Pharisees and Sadducees heard that Jesus was in the area, they decided to test Him to see if He really had been sent by God. They said, "Give us a sign from heaven to prove who You say You are."

Jesus answered, "When you see a beautiful sunset, you say that the next day will be a wonderful day. And when some morning you see an angry-looking sky, you say that it'll be a stormy day. If you can interpret the signs in the sky, why is it so hard for you to interpret the miracles I've done? The problem is that you don't want to accept Me for who I am, so you keep looking for greater and greater miracles. But no greater sign will be given than what God did for Jonah."

Then Jesus got back in the boat with His disciples and crossed to the other side of the lake.

After they had crossed the lake, they were hungry, but the disciples discovered that they had forgotten to take any bread along. Jesus said, "Be careful of the yeast of the Pharisees and Sadducees." They thought He was talking about them forgetting to bring bread. Jesus knew what they were thinking and said, "You have such little spiritual insight. Do you think I'm concerned about your forgetting to bring bread along? Don't you remember that I fed 5,000 men with five pieces of round flatbread and there was food left over? And more recently I fed 4,000 men with seven pieces of round flatbreads, and seven basketfuls of food were left? How come you can't understand that I was not talking about bread or yeast, but about the beliefs of the Pharisees and Sadducees?" Then they understood why He was so concerned (Matt. 16:1-12).

Finally they got to the other side of the lake and landed near Bethsaida. No sooner did they walk into town than people recognized them and brought their sick to Jesus to heal them. One man was blind. Jesus took him by the hand and led him away from the crowd. He put a little of His saliva on the man's closed eyelids and asked him to open his eyes and tell Him what he saw.

The man said, "I see people, but they look like walking trees."

Jesus asked the man to close his eyes, and He touched his eyelids again. He asked him to look straight up.

When the man looked up, he said excitedly, "I can see! Everything is clear!"

Jesus said, "Don't go back into town, but go straight home. And don't tell people you meet along the way what happened. It will draw too much attention to Me at this time" (Mark 8:22-26).

Jesus Questions His Disciples

Then Jesus and His disciples left Galilee and headed north toward Caesarea Philippi. As they were walking along, He asked them, "Who do people say that I am?"

They answered, "Some say that you're John the Baptist raised from the dead. Some say you're Elijah come back from heaven. And still others think you're Jeremiah or one of the other prophets returned to life."

Jesus asked, "Who do you think I am?" Immediately Peter spoke up: "We believe that you are the Messiah, the Son of the living God."

Jesus responded, "Bless you, Simon! You said it with such conviction that it's obvious that you didn't get it from someone else, but that My Father in heaven revealed it to you. While your name is Peter, which means 'rock,' you're just a small stone. I will build the church on Myself, the Rock of God, and all the power of evil will not be able to overcome it. I am giving you, My disciples, the keys to the kingdom of heaven. Whatever you do according to Scripture will be approved by heaven. Anything you do contrary to Scripture will not be approved by heaven."

After this discussion, He warned them not to agitate the people or the religious leaders with the question of who He was.

Also He told His disciples that He must go to Jerusalem and suffer many things at the hands of the leading priests and religious teachers. They would have Him arrested and killed, but three days later He would rise from the grave. Peter pulled Jesus to one side and said, "Don't talk that way! We will never let that happen to You!"

After Jesus rebuked the devil who was influencing Peter, He said, "By taking a stand like that, you would hinder Me from fulfilling My mission. You're looking at things not from God's perspective but from man's point of view."

Turning to the others, Jesus said, "If you really want to be My disciples, you will have to set aside your personal ambitions, shoulder your cross, and follow Me. Anyone who concentrates on saving his own life will lose it. But if he sacrifices himself for my sake, he will find true joy and will be given eternal life. What good will it do if a man gains the whole world and loses his soul? Can he buy eternal life with money? One day the Son of Man will return in the glory of His Father and with the holy angels to reward everyone according to what he has done. Some of you standing here will not die before you will be given a glimpse of My second coming" (Matt. 16:13-28).

Leaving the region, Jesus and His disciples headed back to Galilee, avoiding the more populated areas. This gave Jesus another opportunity to tell His disciples what was going to happen to Him. He said, "The Son of Man will be betrayed and turned over to the Romans, who will kill Him, but three days later He will come back to life."

The disciples still didn't understand what He was talking about, but they hesitated to ask him (Mark 9:30-32).

twelve

Jesus Gives New Insights

About a week later Jesus chose Peter, James, and John to go with Him to the top of a mountain to pray, and left the other disciples with the people. When they reached the top of the mountain, Jesus began to pray. Suddenly He was transfigured before their eyes! His face shone like sunlight, and His robe was dazzling white. Moses and Elijah stood there with Him, talking to Him.

When Peter saw the glory of Jesus, he got so excited that he blurted out, "Lord, let's build three shrines here—one for You, one for Moses, and one for Elijah!" He continued talking but hardly knew what he was saying.

Suddenly an extremely bright cloud appeared over the mountain, and a voice said, "This is My beloved Son, in whom I am well pleased. Listen to Him!" Then the cloud disappeared.

When the three disciples heard that voice, they covered their faces and threw themselves on the ground, scared to death. Then Jesus touched them and said, "Don't be afraid. You may get up now."

When they looked up, they saw no one but Jesus, and He appeared the same as He had before.

As they walked down the mountain, Jesus said to them, "Don't tell anyone what you saw until after My resurrection."

They kept it to themselves as He had asked them to, but they did wonder what Jesus meant by His "resurrection."

So they asked Him, "Why do our religion teachers tell us that Elijah must return from heaven first before the Messiah can come?" Jesus answered, "It's true—Elijah must come first. He's already been here and had a message from heaven. But people didn't listen to him or understand his mission. So they put him in prison, mistreated him, and killed him. And they will do the same sort of thing to the Son of Man, just as the Scripture says." Then they understood that He was talking about John the Baptist (Matt. 17:1-13; Mark 9:2-13).

When they got to the bottom of the mountain, they saw a great crowd of people surrounding the other disciples and the religious teachers, who were arguing with each other. As soon as the people saw Jesus, they ran to greet Him. He made His way to the disciples and asked the religious teachers what they were arguing about.

Just then a man spoke up: "Lord, have mercy on my son and me! He can't speak anymore because he's possessed by an evil spirit. Sometimes it takes hold of him and throws him into the fire or into the water. Sometimes it throws him on the ground, and he begins grinding his teeth and foaming at the mouth. His body becomes as stiff as if he were dead. I asked Your disciples to cast out the evil spirit and heal my son, but they couldn't."

Jesus quietly said to Himself, "How much longer will I have to see such lack of faith?" Then He said to the father, "Bring the boy here."

When the man brought his son, the evil spirit suddenly took hold of the son and threw him to the ground, and he started foaming at the mouth. Jesus asked the father how long this had been going on, to which he replied, "Since he was a child. If you can do something, please have compassion on us!"

Jesus said, "All things are possible to those who believe."

The father cried out, "Lord, I believe! Please help my unbelief!"

Then Jesus rebuked the evil spirit, saying, "Come out of this boy, and don't enter him again!"

The evil spirit let out a shriek, threw the boy into a violent convulsion, and left him. The boy lay there as if he were dead. Many in the crowd said, "He's dead!" Jesus reached down, took the boy by the hand, and helped him up. He was totally healed.

Later when the disciples were in a house alone with Jesus, they asked, "Why couldn't we cast out the evil spirit and heal the boy?"

Jesus replied, "It was because of your lack of faith and of dependence on God. If you have the right kind of faith, even if it's as small as a mustard seed, you can move mountains and tell them to fall into the sea, and they would. But some things, like casting out this evil spirit, will not happen except by fasting and prayer" (Matthew 17:14-21; Mark 9:14-29).

They left that part of Galilee, and Jesus avoided the crowds because He wanted to spend more time with His disciples. Once again He tried to prepare them for what was coming. "It won't be long now," He said, "before the Son of Man will be betrayed, arrested, and killed. But three days later He will rise from the grave."

Temple Taxes

When they got to Capernaum, the Temple tax collectors came to Peter and asked, "Do you and your Teacher pay the required tax for the upkeep of the Temple?"

Peter blurted out, "Of course we do! Let me go into the house and ask Him."

Jesus anticipated His question and said, "Peter, let Me ask you a question: From whom does a king collect taxes—his own family, or the people?"

Without hesitation Peter answered, "From the people, of course!"

Jesus replied, "If that's the case, then the king's family is free of the tax. But let's not offend these men. Go down to the lake, throw in a fishing line, and open the mouth of the first fish you catch. Inside you'll find a silver coin. Take the coin and pay the Temple tax for the two of us" (Matt. 17:22-27).

Jealousy Among the Disciples

After days of traveling, Jesus and His disciples were glad to be in a house for a while. One day at lunch Jesus asked them, "What were you arguing about along the way?" They were all quiet because they had been quarreling about which one of them would be the greatest when Jesus set up His kingdom.

Then Jesus led them out to a hillside and asked them to sit close to Him. He said, "If anyone tries to be first, he will be last and the servant of everyone else." He reached out and took a little child from the crowd, held him in His arms, and said, "Anyone who is as humble and trusting as this little child is considered great. Anyone who accepts and loves a little child in My name, loves Me also and the Father who sent Me."

John said to Jesus, "Teacher, we saw a man using Your name to cast out demons. We told him to stop because he's not one of us."

Jesus replied, "Don't stop him. No one can use My name to cast out demons and then speak evil of Me. Anyone who is not actively against Me is for Me. Even if someone gives you a cup of water in My name, he will not lose his reward. But if anyone causes one of these little ones who believes to lose their faith in Me, he deserves to have a millstone tied around his neck and be thrown into the sea.

"You need to be willing to sacrifice anything that causes you to sin. If it's your hand, cut if off. It's better to go through life with one hand than to have two hands, only to be thrown into the lake of fire. That fire will do its work as thoroughly at the time of judgment as worms eat a dead body or a forest fire burns up trees. If your feet take you where you shouldn't go, cut one off. It's better to go through life with one foot and be given eternal life than to have two feet and end up in the lake of fire, which no one can stop until it consumes everything. If your eyes look at things they shouldn't, take one out. It's better to have one eye and be saved than to have two eyes and be destroyed.

"Everyone's loyalty will be tested, even if it has to be purified by fire. And every sacrifice made for Me has to be seasoned with salt to give it the right flavor. What good is salt if it has no flavor? Sprinkle your lives with salt and live in peace" (Mark 9:33-50).

thirteen

Jesus Goes to Jerusalem

Jesus continued His ministry in Galilee, going from village to village. He had no plans to go to Jerusalem, because the Jewish leaders were already plotting His death. But soon it was time for the Festival of Shelters, and His stepbrothers stopped by and urged Him to go. They said, "Why don't You go to Jerusalem and work some miracles so those who believe in You can see them too? No one who makes the claims that You do should stay away from Jerusalem and hide up here in Galilee. Prove Your claim openly for the world to see!" (They wanted their family respected, not because they believe that He was the Son of God!)

Jesus answered, "Now is not the time for Me to go. But you may go. The religious leaders don't hate you—they hate Me, because I point out their sins and show that what they're doing is wrong. So go ahead. I may come later, but this isn't the right time." So He continued with His ministry in Galilee.

A few days later Jesus decided to go to Jerusalem, not by joining the crowds on the main roads, but by taking the side roads and staying out of public view as much as possible. Meanwhile, the religious leaders kept looking for Him at the weeklong festival, but couldn't find Him. They kept asking if anyone had seen Him, but no one had. There was a lot of discussion among the people about Jesus. Some said, "He's a good man." Others said, "He's a fraud going around deceiving people." No one had the courage to speak favorably about Him to the religious leaders, because they were afraid (John 7:1-13).

Confrontation in the Temple

In the middle of the week Jesus arrived in Jerusalem. Making His way to the Temple, He began teaching the people. As the Jewish religious leaders listened, they were amazed and said among themselves, "Where did He get all His learning when He hasn't studied under us?"

Jesus overheard what they were saying and answered their question: "What I'm teaching is not something I thought up, but what God taught Me. Anyone who is truly willing to do the will of God will know whether what I'm saying is from God or not. Those who love to teach their own ideas are interested in their own glory, but He who wants to honor the one who sent Him will speak truth. Not one of you keeps the law of Moses, no matter how much you talk about it, because you're already planning to kill Me."

The crowd responded, "You're demon-possessed! Who's trying to kill you?"

Jesus looked at the crowd and said, "I healed a man on the Sabbath and you were offended. For what? You think nothing about circumcising on the eighth day even if it falls on the Sabbath, because that's what Moses said you should do. But that wasn't his idea. Circumcision goes back to Abraham, who got it from God. So why should you condemn Me for healing on the Sabbath? Isn't healing a man more important than circumcising? You need to look at the larger picture before you judge someone."

Some of those living in Jerusalem said among themselves, "Isn't this the Man the leaders want to arrest and kill for breaking the Sabbath? Yet here He is speaking in public, and no one tries to stop Him. Maybe our leaders have changed their minds and believe that He is the Messiah after all. But how can that be? We know where He's from, but when the Messiah appears, no one will know where He came from."

Then Jesus called out, "Yes, you know Me and where I'm from, but I didn't come on My own. I came by the authority of the One who sent me. He is always truthful and does what is right. I know Him because I've come from where He is, and he is the One who sent me." The leaders wanted to arrest Him for saying this, but no one laid hands on Him, because His time had not yet come.

People Divided Over Jesus

Many who heard Jesus that day believed that He was the Messiah. "After all," they said, "will the Messiah do any greater miracles than this Man is doing?" When the Jewish religious leaders heard what some people were saying about Jesus, they decided to send for the Temple guards to have Him arrested.

Jesus stated, "I'll be here just a little while longer; then I'll go back to the One who sent Me. You'll look for Me but won't find Me. And where I go, you can't come."

Then the priests and Pharisees said among themselves, "Where is He going that we can't find Him? Maybe He's planning to leave the country and live among the Jews in other countries and teach the people there. What does He mean when He says, 'You'll look for Me and can't find Me,' and 'You can't come where I am'?" So they decided to wait and see before having Him arrested.

On the last day of the festival, Jesus stood at one end of the Temple courtyard and called out, "If anyone is thirsty, let him come to Me and drink. He who believes who I am, out of his heart will flow life-giving water, just as the Scripture says." By this He meant that the Holy Spirit would water their thirsty hearts until they overflowed, alluding to Pentecost, when the Holy Spirit would be given in fuller measure.

When the people heard Jesus call out to them as He did, some said, "There is no question that this Man is a prophet." Others said, "He's the Messiah!" Still others said, "The Messiah won't come from Galilee. The Scripture says that He will come from the royal line of David, from Bethlehem, where David was born." So the people were divided over who Jesus was. And there were some who wanted Jesus arrested, but no one laid a hand on Him. Then the Temple guards who were supposed to arrest Jesus went back to the Jewish leaders and reported what was happening. The priests and Pharisees asked, "Where is He? Why didn't you arrest Him?"

They answered, "We've never heard an ordinary man talk like that. He speaks with such authority."

The priests and Pharisees became angry and said, "Has He deceived you, too? Not one of us believes in Him. What do the people know about the law? They can't even read the Scriptures. Let them be cursed!"

Then Nicodemus, who had talked to Jesus during a late-night interview, spoke up and asked, "Doesn't our law protect the rights of a man and refuses to condemn him without a trial? Shouldn't He be given a hearing to find out what He has done and what He has to say for Himself?"

They answered, "Are you a follower of this Galilean too? Search the Scriptures and see for yourself that no prophet has ever come out of Galilee." The meeting broke up, and everyone went home (John 7:14-53).

Pharisees Set a Trap for Jesus

Toward evening Jesus left the Temple and made His way out of the city to the Mount of Olives to pray. Early the next morning He went back to the Temple and began teaching the people. As He was teaching, the scribes and Pharisees brought a woman to Jesus, whom they had led into adultery. They pushed her in front of Him and said, "Teacher, we caught this woman in the act of adultery. According to Moses' law, she should be stoned. We want You to decide. What do You say?"

They were trying to trap Him into saying something against Moses so they could arrest Him without creating a disturbance. Jesus said nothing, but stooped down and began writing on the pavement stones. The Pharisees kept demanding an answer, but He continued writing. Finally He stood up and said, "Any of you who has never sinned, throw the first stone!" He stooped down again and again traced words on the stones. When they saw what He was writing, one by one they slipped away, beginning with the oldest, until only Jesus and the woman remained in the middle of the crowd.

Then Jesus asked the woman, "What happened to your accusers? Where are they? Have any of them decided to condemn you?"

She answered, "Not one, Lord." Jesus said, "Neither do I condemn you. Go and sin no more" (John 8:1-11).

Jesus' Ancestry Questioned

Jesus turned to the crowd and said, "I am the light of the world. If you follow Me, you will no longer have to grope your way in darkness, but will have a light to guide you to eternal life."

By now some of the Pharisees had rejoined the crowd. They shouted, "What you're saying about Yourself is not true!"

Jesus responded, "What I'm saying is true. I know where I came from and where I'm going, but you don't even want to know. You're judging Me by my outward appearance. I pass judgment on no one except in conjunction with My Father, and My judgment is correct. The law says that if two witnesses agree on something, what they say should be accepted as true. I am one witness, and my Father is the other."

They asked, "Who is Your Father? Nobody seems to know."

Jesus answered, "If you don't know who I am, how could you know who My Father is? If you know who I am, then you will know who My Father is, too." Jesus had this conversation with the Pharisees near the Temple treasury where the guards were stationed, but they did not arrest Him, because the time for that had not yet come.

Later that day He had another conversation with the Pharisees. He said to them, "Soon I'll be going away, and you will be left to die in your sins because you can't come where I'm going."

They said to each other, "Do you think He's planning to kill Himself? What else could He mean when He says, 'Where I go, you can't come'?"

Jesus responded, "Your heart is in this world. My heart is in the world above. That's why I said, 'You will die in your sins,' because you don't believe who I am."

They said, "Tell us who You are." Jesus replied, "I told you. I could tell you much more, but I say only what the Father tells Me to say, and what He says is true."

They still didn't understand that Jesus was talking not about an earthly father but about His Father in heaven.

Then Jesus said to them, "After you condemn the Son of Man and He is lifted up high, then you will know who I am and that I did nothing on My own, but only what My Father told Me. He who sent Me has not abandoned Me, because I do those things that please Him."

Many who heard Him that day believed in Him (John 8:12-30).

Then Jesus turned to the crowd and said, "If you continue to believe in Me and obey My teachings, then you are truly My disciples. Soon you will learn even more truth about Me, and the truth will set you free."

The crowd responded, "But we are a free people. We are the descendants of Abraham and have never been enslaved by anyone. So what do you mean, 'The truth will set you free'?"

Jesus answered, "Anyone who sins is a slave, and as you know, a slave is not part of the family. A son is part of the family. I am the Father's Son, so if the Son sets you free, you will indeed be free. Yes, you are the descendants of Abraham, and yet some of you are making plans to kill Me because My words have not found a place in your hearts. I'm telling you what I know and what I saw when I was with my Father. But you are listening to a different father."

They said, "Our father is Abraham."

Jesus replied, "If you were the children of Abraham, you would act like Abraham. But you're planning to kill Me. Abraham wouldn't do that. The truth I'm sharing with you I got from God. Abraham wouldn't act like this. You're listening not to him but to a different father."

They responded, "We know who our father is, but You don't, because You were born illegitimately. Our real Father is God."

Jesus said, "If God were your Father, you would respect and honor Me, because I have come from God. I didn't come here on My own. He's the one who sent Me. Why can't you understand what I'm saying? It's because you're not really listening to Me—you're listening to the devil and doing what he wants you to do. So he's your real father. He had murder in his heart from the beginning and has always hated the truth about Me. There's no truth in him. He lies and is the father of all lies. You don't believe Me because you're listening to him. Which one of you can accuse Me of lying? So if I'm telling you the truth, why don't you believe Me? Anyone who has God as his Father would gladly listen to the words of God. Because you're not listening, you can't be the children of God."

The Jewish religious leaders spoke up, "You're a crafty Samaritan, controlled by the devil."

Jesus replied, "I am not demon-possessed. I'm here to honor My Father, but you don't even give Me the respect you give a stranger. I'm not here for My own glory—God wants to honor Me. Let Him be the judge. Let Me tell you that anyone who listens to Me and obeys My teaching will never die!"

They laughed, "Now we know that You're demon-possessed. Abraham died, and so did the prophets, yet You say, 'Anyone who obeys My teachings will never die.' Are You greater than Abraham and the prophets, who never claimed to have the power of life? Who do You think You are?"

Jesus answered, "If I claim to have this power and boast about Myself, it means nothing. But it is the Father who says these things about Me. He is the God you claim to worship, yet you don't know Him. But I do. If I denied knowing Him, I would be lying, as you are. I know Him and obey Him. Abraham looked forward to My coming and rejoiced. He saw My day and was glad."

They sneered, "You're not even 50 years old, so how can You say that Abraham saw your day?"

Jesus answered, "I existed before Abraham was born."

Then they went to get some rocks to stone Him to death. But when they came back looking for Him, they couldn't find Him, because He had hidden Himself from them. When He left the Temple, He walked right past them, but they didn't see Him (John 8:31-59).

fourteen

Travels, Miracles, and Stories

As Jesus and His disciples left Jerusalem to head north to Galilee, they saw a man whom the people knew had been blind from birth. His disciples asked, "Teacher, was this man born blind because of his parents' sins or his future sins?"

Jesus answered, "Neither one. But his condition will give God an opportunity to show His power. This is what I was sent here for—to do God's work while I can, because I don't have much time left. Soon the night will come, and the day will end. But while I'm here, I'm God's light to the world."

Jesus asked His disciples to bring the blind man to Him. When he came, Jesus used a little saliva to make a tiny bit of mud and put it on the blind man's eyes. Then He told the man, "Go to the Pool of Siloam and wash the mud off your eyes."

The man did as he was told, and when he opened his eyes, he could see. He ran all the way home, praising God!

His neighbors and those who knew him asked, "Isn't he the one who was born blind and sat by the road begging?"

Others said, "Yes, he's the one!" Still others said, "No, he's not. He just looks like him."

The man shouted, "I am the one!"

So they asked him, "How did this happen? Who healed you?"

He answered, "The man they call Jesus used His saliva to make a little mud and put it on my eyes. Then He told me to go to the Pool of Siloam and wash it off, and when I did, I could see!"

They asked, "Where is He?"

He answered, "I don't know."

So they took the man to the local Pharisees, because Jesus had healed him on the Sabbath and had made mud to do it. The Pharisees asked him how the healing had happened.

The man answered, "Jesus put a little mud on my eyes and told me to wash it off. When I did, I could see."

They said, "This Jesus could not be sent by God, because He broke the Sabbath."

Those who brought the man said, "But if He sinned by breaking the Sabbath, how could He work such a miracle?"

So they disagreed among themselves.

Then the Pharisees asked the man, "What do you have to say? Who do you think this Jesus is?"

The man said, "I believe He's a prophet of God."

The Pharisees didn't believe that the man was born blind. So they sent for his parents and asked, "Is this your son? Was he born blind?"

His parents answered, "This is our son, and he was born blind. But we don't know what happened to make him see or who healed him. He's old enough—ask him." They answered this way because they were afraid of the religious leaders, who had announced that anyone who believed Jesus was the Messiah would be barred from the synagogue. That's why they said, "He is of age—ask him."

The Pharisees called the man back in and asked him again, "Tell us the truth. What happened to make you see? Give God the glory, not this man Jesus, because we know He's a sinner."

The man answered, "I don't know whether He's a sinner or not. All I know is that once I was blind, and now I see!"

They asked again, "Tell us what He did to make you see."

The man answered, "I told you once. Didn't you hear what I said? Why do you want to hear it again? Are you interested in becoming His disciples?"

The Pharisees glared at him, then said, "You might be His disciple, but we are disciples of Moses. We know that God worked through Moses, but as for this Man, we don't even know who His father is or much of anything about Him."

The man replied, "That's amazing! You say you don't know anything about Him, yet He gave sight to someone born blind. We know that God doesn't work through sinners, but through those who worship Him and obey Him. Never in our history has there been a case in which someone gave sight to a man born blind. If this Man hadn't been close to God, He couldn't have healed me."

They said, "You're a sinner and were conceived in sin—that's why you were born blind. And *you* are trying to teach *us?*" Then they threw him out of the synagogue.

When Jesus heard what had happened, He went looking for the man.

When He found him, He said, "Would you like to meet the Son of Man?"

The man responded, "Yes, of course I would!"

Jesus said, "You're looking at Him. He's the one talking to you."

The man exclaimed, "Lord, You sound like the one who healed me! I believe You are who You say You are!" Then he fell on his knees and worshipped Him.

When he got up, Jesus said, "My presence in this world judges people for what they are. I give sight to those who want to know Me, and point out to those who think they can see that they are blind."

The nearby Pharisees heard this and spoke up: "Are you saying that we're blind?"

Jesus answered, "If you admitted that you couldn't see, you wouldn't be guilty, but because you keep insisting that you can see, your guilt remains" (John 9).

Jesus, the Good Shepherd

Jesus continued, "Let Me assure you: Anyone who enters the sheep pen by climbing over the wall instead of going through the gate is a thief and a robber. The shepherd goes through the gate. The gatekeeper opens the gate for him, and the sheep recognize his voice and come. He calls each one of them by name, and they follow him out to pasture. They won't follow a stranger, but will run from him, because they don't know his voice."

The Pharisees didn't understand what He was talking about, so He explained it to them. "I am the gate into God's sheep pen. All those who came before Me claiming to be the Messiah were thieves and robbers. God's sheep didn't listen to them. It's true—I am the gate. Those who come into God's fold through Me will be led to green pastures and be saved. Thieves and robbers steal and kill sheep. I have come that the sheep might have eternal life. Also, I am the good shepherd. A good shepherd is willing to die for his sheep. When a hired man sees a wolf coming, he runs because he's not the shepherd. So the wolf attacks the sheep, kills one, and scatters the rest. A hired man runs because he's interested not in protecting the sheep, but in saving himself.

"I am the good shepherd. I know My sheep, and they know Me. The Father knows that I'm ready to die for the sheep, and I know how much He loves them. I have other sheep that are not of this fold—I must bring them, too. They will listen to My voice and will come, and there will be one fold and one shepherd. The Father loves Me, for He knows that I too am willing to die for the sheep. I will lay down My life and then take it back again. This is what My Father has asked Me to do."

When the people heard this, they were again divided. Some said, "He's mad. He's possessed by a demon. Why should we listen to Him?"

Others said, "He doesn't sound like a man possessed by a demon. Can a demon-possessed man open the eyes of someone born blind?" (John 10:1-21).

Jesus Talks About Attitude

After this, Jesus left Galilee and headed back south toward Jerusalem, passing through Samaria on the way. He sent James and John ahead to a Samaritan village to let people know He was coming. But the people didn't want Him to come, because they knew He would only be passing through on His way to Jerusalem.

When the two disciples saw the people's attitude, they went back to Jesus and said, "Lord, these people don't want You to come because they know we're on our way to Jerusalem. What do You want us to do? We ought to call down fire from heaven, as Elijah did, and burn them all up!"

Jesus rebuked them, saying, "What kind of spirit is that? I have not come to destroy people, but to save them."

So they passed by Samaria and went on to the next village.

On the way a man stopped Jesus and said, "Lord, I'm willing to be Your disciple and follow You."

Jesus asked, "Are you sure? Foxes have dens and birds have nests, but I have no place of My own, not even a place to lay My head."

Then Jesus turned to another man and said, "Come, be My disciple."

The man responded similar to a previous one, "I'll be happy to be your disciple, but first let me go home to make arrangements to bury my father."

Jesus said, "Let those who are not interested in Me, who are spiritually dead, make the arrangements. A disciple's first obligation is decide to follow Me and then do what he can to advance the kingdom of God."

Another man spoke up: "Lord, I'll be Your disciple and follow You, but first let me say goodbye to my family."

Jesus replied, "Anyone who puts his hand to the plow and keeps looking back is not worthy of Me and is not fit for the kingdom of God" (Luke 9:51-62).

Jesus Needed More Help

Then Jesus selected 70 additional disciples and sent them out in pairs to go ahead of Him to towns and villages that He planned to visit. He said to them, "The harvest is great, but the laborers are few. Pray that God will send more laborers into the field to help you. Now be on your way. You'll be like lambs among wolves. But don't worry. Don't take along a lot of money, not even an extra pair of sandals or a beggar's bag. Don't stop and talk to everyone you meet along the way, but remember to focus on your mission.

"As I told others, if people invite you to stay with them, give it the blessing of peace as you enter the house. If the people are peaceful, the blessing will stay. If they are not, the blessing will come back to you. When you enter a village or a town, don't keep moving from house to house. It will leave the wrong impression. Stay in one place until your work is finished. Eat what they serve you, and thank them for their kindness. Heal the sick, and as you do, tell the people that the kingdom of God has come.

"If the town doesn't want you to stay, get your things, and as you leave, shake the dust off your sandals. Say to the people, 'You're rejecting not us but the kingdom of God.' Let me tell you, the wicked people of Sodom will receive more consideration in the judgment than the townspeople who reject you."

Then Jesus said, "Condemnation awaits cities such as Korazin and Bethsaida. If the miracles I did there had been done in the Phoenician cities of Tyre and Sidon, the people would have repented in sackcloth with ashes on their heads. That's why Tyre and Sidon will be shown more mercy in the judgment than these cities. Will Capernaum be exalted because I made it My second home? No, it will be even worse off."

Turning back to the 70, He said, "Those who listen to you are listening to Me. And those who reject you are rejecting Me and the one who sent Me."

When the 70 came back from their mission, their hearts were overflowing with joy. They said to Jesus, "Lord, even the demons obeyed us when we used Your name!"

Jesus was thrilled to hear what they had done, and said, "I saw that Satan's fall will be like a bolt of lightning striking the ground. I have given you power to cast out demons, which are like snakes and scorpions. Don't be afraid—if you stay close to Me, they can't hurt you. However, don't rejoice in your power over demons. Instead, rejoice in helping Me and that your names are registered in heaven."

Then Jesus, filled with the Holy Spirit, expressed His joy to His Father, saying, "Thank You, Father, for helping these men. Truly You are the Lord of heaven and earth. You didn't share Your power with those who think they are wise and know so much, but with those of childlike faith. Father, You always do things right. And You have given Me authority over everything, because no one knows Me as You do and no one knows You as I do, except those who listen and with whom I share it."

When Jesus was alone with His disciples, He said to them, "How privileged you are to see the things you have seen! Many prophets and kings have longed to see and hear the things you have, but they didn't have that privilege" (Luke 10:1-24).

The Good Samaritan

About this time an expert in religious law tested Jesus with a question. "Teacher," he said, "what must I do to receive eternal life?"

Jesus answered, "What does the law say, and how do you understand it?"

He replied, "We should love the Lord our God with all our heart, soul, mind, and strength, and our neighbor as ourselves."

Jesus responded, "That's right. Do it, and you will have eternal life."

The man wanted to justify his exclusiveness, so he asked, "How do I know who is my neighbor?"

Jesus answered, "Let Me tell you what happened recently. A Jewish man left Jerusalem to go to Jericho. On the way robbers attacked him. They beat him up, took his money, stripped him of his clothes, and left him lying by the side of the road almost dead. A Jewish priest came along on his way to Jerusalem. As he looked ahead, he could see an injured man lying there needing help, but he crossed to the other side and kept going. Later a Levite, one of the Temple assistants, came along. He saw the man, stopped to look at him, but also left him lying there.

"Then a Samaritan came along, riding on a donkey. When he saw the injured Jew, he felt sorry for him and decided to help him. He got off his donkey, knelt down beside the man, used wine and oil to clean his wounds, bandaged him up, and helped him get on the donkey. He took him to a nearby inn and took care of him all night. The next morning he gave the innkeeper some money and said, 'Please care for this man for me, and whatever else it costs, I'll pay you the next time I come back.' Which one of these three men would you say was a neighbor to the injured man?"

The expert in the law answered, "The one who showed mercy and cared for him."

Jesus replied, "You have your answer. Go and do likewise" (Luke 10:25-37).

Jesus Returns to Jerusalem

Jesus and His disciples made their way back toward Jerusalem, stopping at Bethany, a village in which Martha and her sister Mary lived. Martha was glad to see them and welcomed them into her home. Mary never missed an opportunity to sit at Jesus' feet to listen to what He had to say. But Martha rushed around, trying to get something to eat for 13 hungry men. Finally she went to Jesus and complained, "Lord, don't You care that my sister has left me to do all this work alone? Tell her to help me."

Jesus looked lovingly at Martha and said, "Martha, Martha, you are so kind and helpful, yet you're overly concerned about details. You go to great lengths to make us comfortable and feed us. But sometimes there are more important things to be concerned about. Mary needs My help. She did the right thing to come to Me. No one can ever take this experience away from her" (Luke 10:38-42).

From Bethany, Jesus and His disciples went to Jerusalem for the Festival of Dedication, also called the Festival of Lights, or Hanukkah. As Jesus was walking along Solomon's Colonnade, which was attached to the Temple, the Jewish leaders surrounded Him and said, "If You're the Messiah, tell us how much longer You are going to keep us in suspense."

Jesus answered, "I've already told you, but you don't believe Me. The proof is in what I do, and that I do it in My Father's name. Yet you still don't believe Me, because you're not part of My flock. My sheep hear My voice and know Me, and I know them and they follow Me. I will give them eternal life, and they will never die. No one can take them away from Me. My Father loves them too, and He has more power than anyone else, so no one can take them away from Him. And I and My Father are one."

Then the Jewish leaders went to get some rocks to stone Jesus to death for what He had said, as they had tried to do before. When they returned, Jesus faced them and asked, "I have done nothing but good to people, all at My Father's direction. For which of these things are you going to stone Me?"

They answered, "We're not going to stone You for any good thing, but for blasphemy because You claim to be the Son of God and equal with Him."

Jesus responded, "Didn't God say, 'You look up to judges as if they were gods, but all My children are sons of the Most High'? You know that what the Scripture says is true. So why do you accuse Me of blasphemy when I say that the Father has sent Me into the world and that I am his Son? You wouldn't have to believe in Me if you hadn't seen Me doing My Father's work. But at least believe that the work I do is from God. Then you'll know that the Father is in Me, that I am in the Father, and that We are one."

Then they grabbed Jesus, but He slipped out of their hands and went on His way. From Jerusalem He headed north to the Jordan River in the province of Peraea, where John the Baptist had first preached and baptized. Many followed Him and said to each other, "John didn't work miracles, but what he said about this Jesus is true." And many of them believed that He was the Messiah (John 10:22-42).

Jesus Talks About Prayer

Early one morning Jesus' disciples found Him in a secluded place praying. When He finished, they said, "Lord, teach us to pray as John taught his disciples to pray."

Jesus responded, "I've mentioned this to you before. When you pray, pray something like this: Our Father, may Your name be honored in all we do. May Your kingdom come, and may we do Your will here on earth as it is done in heaven. Provide for our daily needs, and help us to forgive others as You forgive us. Don't let us be tempted beyond what we can bear, but deliver us from the evil one."

Then Jesus continued: "Let Me explain what praying is like. Suppose you had a close friend and went to his house at midnight to borrow some bread. You would knock on his door and say to him, 'A friend of mine came unexpectedly to visit, and we're out of bread. Could I borrow three loaves?'

"Your friend would lean his head out of his bedroom window and quietly say, 'Not now. The door is locked, and the children are in bed sound asleep. I can't rummage through the house looking for extra bread.'

"Even though your friend doesn't sound as though he will help you, if you keep asking he will open the door and give you what you need because he is your friend.

"So keep on asking, and you'll be given. Keep on seeking, and you'll find. Keep on knocking, and the door will open. Everyone who asks, receives. He who seeks, finds. And to him who knocks, the door will open.

"If one of your children asks for bread, would you give him a stone? If he asks for a fish, would you give him a snake? If he asks for an egg, would you give him a scorpion? If sinful people know how to give what's good to their children, how much more is your heavenly Father ready to give you what you need and to send the Holy Spirit to those who ask Him!" (Luke 11:1-13).

Jesus Talks About Heart Religion

Jesus continued: "No one lights a lamp and then hides it or puts it under a basket. He puts it on a lampstand so that everyone who comes into the house can see. Your eyes are like lamps. When you think good thoughts, your eyes let God's light into your soul; but when you think evil, your eyes shut out God's light, and your soul is left in darkness. So make sure that what you have in your heart is light and not darkness. If you're filled with light, there will be no dark corners, and your life will shine like a lamp to help others see."

When Jesus finished, a Pharisee invited Him home to dinner. Jesus followed the man home, went into the house, and sat down to eat. The Pharisee was surprised that Jesus didn't first go through the ritual of washing His hands like the Pharisees, but he said nothing.

Jesus began to speak, "I know how exact the Pharisees are about the ritual of washing hands and that their dishes and cups are clean. But they don't worry about the greed and wicked thoughts in their hearts. How foolish can they be! The same God who made the outside of us also made the inside. Feed the poor and be kind and gentle to others, and you'll be clean inside and out.

"A terrible day will come for Pharisees, who so carefully tithe the smallest income from garden produce, but neglect justice and living the love of God. Of course you should tithe, but don't forget what's most important. They love their seats of honor in the synagogue and the respectful greetings they get in the marketplace. But it won't be that way in the judgment. In the sight of heaven, they're like unmarked graves in a field that people walk on without knowing it."

Then one of the teachers of religious law spoke up, "Teacher, when You talk about the Pharisees this way, You make us look bad."

Jesus replied, "You're right. The problem is that some teachers of the law do the same thing. They load people down with many religious requirements, yet they do nothing to help them. They build monuments to the prophets, some of whom their ancestors killed. Yet they say that what our forefathers did in those situations was right, which means they're ready to do the same thing.

"God knew this would happen when He said, 'I will send them prophets and leaders. Some they will kill, and others they will persecute.' The shedding of blood, such as has been done since the killing of righteous Abel and the prophets right down to the murdering of the prophet Zechariah by the altar in the Temple, will be done again by this evil generation.

"Teachers of religious law are no different from the Pharisees. The key to unlocking the Scriptures is at their disposal, but they won't acknowledge it. They don't understand the kingdom of God, and you try to keep others from understanding it."

After the meal Jesus thanked His host and left. The Pharisees and teachers were furious. From that time on, they took every opportunity to attack Jesus with hostile questions, trying to trip Him into saying something for which they could arrest Him (Luke 11:33-54).

Jesus Talks About Values

Meanwhile, the crowds following Jesus grew so large that the people were almost crushing each other. One day Jesus turned to His disciples and said, "Be careful of the yeast of the Pharisees, which is hypocrisy. They pretend to serve God while serving themselves. The time is coming when everything being done will be uncovered; every secret sin will be made public. Whatever is said in the dark will be brought to light, and whatever is whispered in secret meetings will be shouted from the rooftops.

"You're not only My disciples, but I consider you My friends. Don't be afraid of those who want to kill you. They can only destroy your body, but they can't take anything else away from you. What you need to be afraid of is losing your love for your heavenly Father, who has power over body and soul and can destroy both in the final fires of hell. Let Me ask you a question: How much are five sparrows worth? Not much, for you can buy them for pennies. Yet God knows when one of them falls from a tree. He even knows the number of hairs on your head. So don't be afraid— God loves you. You're of more value to Him than a skyful of sparrows.

"Let me assure you that whoever acknowledges Me publicly as his Lord, I will acknowledge him as belonging to Me before God's angels. But if anyone publicly denies Me, I have no choice but to publicly deny him before God's angels. However, if anyone says something against Me and then repents, he will be forgiven. But if he rejects the Holy Spirit, there is no other way to reach him, so he cannot be forgiven.

"Now when they take you to the synagogue for trial or before rulers and authorities, don't worry what you're going to say, because the Holy Spirit will tell you what to say."

Someone from the crowd spoke up, "Teacher, tell my brother to divide equally the inheritance our parents left us."

Jesus replied, "Friend, I'm not an earthly judge. Judges need to arbitrate such things."

Then He said to the crowd, "Be careful about becoming greedy. Life is more than money and possessions. Let Me tell you about a rich man who owned a large farm. Year after year the land produced a great harvest, filling the man's barns. As he thought about it, he said to himself, 'I know what I'll do: I'll tear down my old barns and build bigger ones. Then I can store enough grain for years to come. And I can sit back and say to myself: Take life easy. Eat, drink, and have a good time.' But God said, 'You fool. Tonight you will die. Then who will get everything you worked so hard for?' That's what happens to those who store up wealth and don't know God."

Jesus Talks About Faith

Then Jesus turned to His disciples and said, "Don't worry so much about everyday things, such as food, clothes, and the needs of your body. Life is more than food and clothes. Look at the birds. They don't sow or reap, nor do they store their food in barns. Your heavenly Father feeds them. You're much more valuable than birds! Worrying can't add an inch to your height or an hour to your life. If you can't do little things like that, why worry so much?

"Look at the flowers in the fields. See how they grow? They don't choose their colors or make their clothes, yet Solomon in all his glory was not dressed as beautifully as they are. Now, if God cares so much about the flowers, which are here today and gone tomorrow, don't you think that He cares that much more about you?

"You have such little faith. Take one day at a time. People think so much about food and clothes and so little about God. Your heavenly Father knows that you need these things. Make His kingdom first in your life, and your daily needs will fall into line. You're His little flock. Don't be so afraid. It's your Father's pleasure to bring you into His kingdom.

"So be generous. Sell what you don't need, and use the money to feed the poor. That's like putting money into the bank of heaven where it's safe. There are no thieves there and no moths to destroy your clothes. Where your money is, that's where your heart will be" (Luke 12:1-34).

Jesus continued: "Be like servants who are dressed, waiting for their master to return from the wedding with his bride. Their lamps are lit, and they're ready to open the door as soon as he knocks. He will be delighted to see his servants ready and waiting. He will seat them, put on an apron, and serve them. He may come back from the wedding late at night or early the next morning. Blessed are those servants who are ready and waiting for him.

"If a homeowner knew exactly when a thief would come, he would stay awake and not let his house be broken into. So stay awake and be ready, for the Son of Man will come when least expected."

Then Peter asked, "Lord, are these parables for us or for everyone?"

Jesus answered, "What I said is for all My servants. But let me ask you a question. Who is a faithful and wise servant? It's one whom the master can trust and to whom he gives the responsibility to manage his household and feed his family while he's gone. When he returns and finds that his servant has done well, he will put him in charge of all he has. But if that servant says to himself, 'My master will be gone for some time,' and begins mistreating those under him, throwing parties for his friends, and getting drunk, his master will come back when he least expects it. He will be given a public whipping and be dismissed for being unfaithful, because he knew what he was supposed to do but didn't do it. But those servants who didn't know what their master expected and did that will be given a lighter punishment. To whom much is given, much is expected, and to whom much is entrusted, even more is expected.

"I have come to light a fire on earth, and how I wish that fire were already lit! But I must first be baptized with a baptism of suffering, and I'm distressed over what I must go through until it's finished. Do you think I've come to usher in an era of peace? No, My coming will actually bring division. In a family of five, three might be for Me and two against Me. Fathers will oppose sons, and sons, fathers. It will be the same with mothers and daughters, mothers-in-law and daughters-in-law."

Then Jesus turned to the crowd and said, "When you see dark clouds come out of the west, you say, 'It's going to rain,' and you're right. When the wind comes from the south, you say, 'It's going to be a hot day,' and it will be. How can you be so sure about the weather and so uncertain about Me? Why can't you make up your minds and do what's right? Suppose on the way to court you meet the one who accuses you. You should settle things with him before you go any further. Once you're before the judge, he might find you guilty and turn you over to an officer to take you to jail. You won't be let out until you've paid every last penny you owe" (Luke 12:35-59).

sixteen

Jesus Continues Teaching the People

About this time Jesus was told that Pilate had ordered some pilgrims from Galilee killed while they were offering sacrifices in the Temple. When Jesus heard it, He said, "Don't you think that these Galileans must have been terrible sinners for this to happen to them? No, not so. But one thing is sure: Unless you change your ways and stop judging people, you too will lose your life. How about these 18 men who died when the tower in Siloam collapsed and fell on them? Were they the worst people in Jerusalem? No, not so. But unless you repent, you too will perish."

Then Jesus continued teaching, saying, "A certain landowner had a special fig tree planted in his orchard. After it took root and grew, he came to see if it had any fruit. But as many times as he came, he never found any. One day he said to his servant in charge of the orchard, 'I've waited for three years for this tree to produce some fruit, but it still hasn't. Cut it down. It's only taking up space and wasting good soil.' His servant answered, 'Sir, let's see what it will do this year. I'll dig around it, fertilize it, and if it still doesn't produce fruit, then I'll cut it down.' And the landowner agreed."

Jesus Explains

Jesus was teaching in the synagogue one Sabbath when He saw a woman with a spinal condition, who was so bent over that she couldn't straighten up. She had been that way for 18 years. He called to her, and when she came, He touched her, saying, "Woman, you are healed."

Instantly she stood up straight and began praising God.

When the leader of the synagogue saw this, he became angry because Jesus had done this on the Sabbath. He said to the people, "There are six days in the week to come to be healed. It shouldn't be done on the Sabbath."

Jesus said, "That's being hypocritical, and what you're telling the people isn't right. Don't you untie your ox or donkey on the Sabbath and lead it out for water? This woman is a daughter of Abraham, whom Satan has controlled for 18 years. Shouldn't I untie her on the Sabbath?"

Those who opposed Him had nothing to say, and the people began praising God for what Jesus had done.

Jesus continued teaching, saying, "What is the kingdom of God like? What should I compare it to? It's like a tiny mustard seed that a man plants in his garden. It sprouts and grows into a large mustard plant. The birds think it's a small tree and build their nests there.

"What else can I compare the kingdom of God to? It's like yeast that a woman puts in bread dough to make it rise. It permeates every bit of the dough, and soon it's ready for baking."

As Jesus made His way toward Jerusalem, He stopped in villages here and there, teaching the people as He went. In one of the villages someone asked, "Lord, how many will be saved and get to heaven—a lot or just a few?"

Jesus answered, "The door into heaven is narrow. So do all you can to get in. Many look forward to getting in, but once the Master of the house locks the door, it will be too late. Then you'll stand outside, knocking and pleading, 'Lord, please open the door!'

"But He will say, 'I don't recognize you.'

"You will beg, 'But we ate and talked with You when You were teaching in our villages and on our streets.'

"He will declare, 'I'm telling you that I don't recognize you. Please leave. You belong with those who don't know Me.'

"Then you will grind your teeth in pain when you see Abraham, Isaac, Jacob, and the prophets in the kingdom, and you're outside. Other people from all over the world will take their places in the kingdom. The first will be last, and the last will be first."

Jesus Stands Firm

Later that day some Pharisees said to Jesus, "You'd better leave the province of Galilee and be on your way to Jerusalem, because Herod wants to kill You."

Jesus answered, "Go tell that fox that I will keep on casting out demons and healing people today and tomorrow. On the third day I'll finish My work and leave. It wouldn't do for a prophet to be killed away from Jerusalem."

Then Jesus changed the subject, saying, "Jerusalem, Jerusalem, you have killed God's prophets and stoned those who were sent to you. How many times have I longed to gather your people together as a hen gathers her chicks under her wings, but you wouldn't let Me! Soon your Temple will be left empty, and you won't see Me again until I return in glory. But then it will be too late to say, 'Bless the one who comes in the name of the Lord' " (Luke 13).

Sabbath Lunch

Now it so happened that a leader of the Pharisees invited Jesus to his house for Sabbath lunch. Some among the guests were watching Jesus very closely to see what He would do, because a man whose arms and legs were very swollen was there. Jesus turned to the Pharisees and experts in religious law and asked, "Is it lawful to heal on the Sabbath?"

When they didn't answer, Jesus healed the man. Then He turned back to them and asked, "If your ox or donkey falls into a ditch on the Sabbath, don't you pull it out? What if that happened to your son—wouldn't you pull him out?" Still no one answered.

Jesus noticed that some of the guests had quickly taken their seats near the head of the table. He said, "If you're invited to a wedding, don't rush to take the best seats in the house, because someone more important might have been invited. When the host notices him, he will have to ask you to give up your seat. That will really be embarrassing, because you'll have to go to the back of the room and take whatever seat is left. So sit in the back, and when the host sees you, he'll come and say, 'Friend, I have a better place for you. Come and sit up here.' Then you'll be honored in the eyes of all who are there. He who thinks he's great will be humbled, and he who humbles himself will be honored."

Then Jesus turned to His host and said, "When you plan a luncheon or dinner, don't invite just your friends, relatives, church members, or rich neighbors. Invite some poor people and those with disabilities. Invite some who can't invite you back. That will give you a good feeling, and at the resurrection God will reward you."

One of the guests remarked, "How fortunate is the man whom God will invite to eat with Him in the kingdom!"

Jesus responded by telling this story: "A certain rich man planned a great feast and decided to invite his neighbors and friends. When everything was ready, he sent his servant to those who had received the invitation, to tell them to come because everything was ready. But they all had excuses. One said, 'I just decided to buy a piece of property, and I have to go and look at it again. Please excuse me.' Another said, 'I just bought five teams of oxen, and I have to try them out. Please excuse me.' Still another said, 'I just got married—I can't possibly come. Please excuse me.'

"So the servant came back and told his master what his neighbors and friends had said. The master was furious and said to his servant, 'Go quickly up and down the streets and alleys, and invite anyone you see—the poor, the disabled, and the blind.' Soon the servant came back and reported, 'Master, I did what you said, but there's still room.' The master said, 'Go to the communities outside the city, along the highways and country roads, and urge people to come, because I want a full house. None of those who turned down my invitation will be allowed in.' "

Discipleship

Great crowds followed Jesus wherever He went. Turning to them, He said, "If you want to follow Me, you need to put Me ahead of your father, mother, wife, children, brothers and sisters, and even your own life, or you can't be My disciple. If you're not willing to carry that cross for Me, you're not worthy to be My disciple.

"Which one of you, planning to build a house, doesn't first sit down to figure out the cost to see if you have enough money to finish it? If you lay the foundation and then run out of money, your neighbors will walk by your place, smile, and say to each other, 'He's the man who didn't count the cost and ran out of money!'

"What king would go to war without first sitting down with his generals to see if with 10,000 troops they can defeat the king coming against them with 20,000 troops? If they don't think they can, they will send a delegation to the other king while he is still a great way off, to ask for terms of peace.

"So no one can be My disciple until he first thinks things through and is willing to give up everything to follow Me.

"Salt is good for seasoning, but if it loses its flavor, what is it good for? You can't even use it to enrich the soil or to mix it with manure to fertilize your garden. That's why people throw it out onto the roadway. If you have ears to hear, then listen to what I've just said" (Luke 14).

seventeen

Jesus Talks About God's Love

It was mostly tax collectors and those living in open sin who came to listen to Jesus. So the Pharisees and the teachers of religious law did all they could to discredit His ministry. They said, "This man associates with the worst kind of people and even eats with them. How can He be the Messiah?"

Jesus responded with these parables: "What would you do if you had 100 sheep and one of them went astray? Wouldn't you leave the other 99 and go looking for the one lost sheep until you found it? And when you found it, you would lay it across your shoulders and come back singing. Then you would tell your neighbors and friends that you had found the sheep that was lost, and they would rejoice with you. That's the way it is in heaven. There is more joy over one sinner who comes back to God than over 99 good people who are safe.

"What would a woman who had 10 silver coins and lost one of them do? Wouldn't she light a lamp and sweep every part of the house until she found it? And when she found it, she would tell her friends and neighbors, 'I found the silver coin that I had lost!' And they too would rejoice with her. That's how it is with the angels in heaven who rejoice over each sinner who was lost and is found."

Jesus continued, "A certain man had two sons. One day the younger said to his father, 'Father, give me my share of the inheritance.' So his father divided his estate between his two sons. A few days later the young son got his things together and left. He went to a neighboring country and there squandered his wealth in wild living.

"About then a famine hit that little country. The son couldn't get a job, and soon began to starve. So he went out to a local farmer and begged for a job. The farmer hired him to take care of his pigs. The young man was so hungry that even what the pigs ate began to look good to him, because the farmer didn't feed him. Finally he came to his senses and said to himself, 'Back home every servant can eat as much as he wants and there's food left over. Here I am starving to death! I know what I'll do. I'll go home and say to my father, 'Father, I have sinned against heaven and you. I'm no longer worthy to be your son. Please hire me as one of your servants.'''

"As weak as he was, he left for home the same day. When he was still some distance from the house, his father spotted him. His great heart of love went out to his son, and he ran to meet him. He hugged and kissed him and welcomed him home. His son said, 'Father, I have sinned against heaven and you. I'm not worthy to be your son.'

"He never finished the rest of it, because his father stopped him and said to one of the servants who also came running, 'Quick, get my best robe for him and the family ring and my own sandals! Then kill the calf we have been fattening. We have to celebrate, because I thought my son was dead, but he's alive! He was lost but has been found!' And they began to celebrate.

"Meanwhile, the older son, who had been working in the field, came home and heard music. When he looked in, he saw dancing. He called one of the servants out and asked him what the celebration was all about. The servant said, 'Your brother is back! And your father asked us to kill the fattened calf and celebrate his safe return.'

"When the older brother heard this, he got angry and refused to go into the house. So his father came out and begged him to join the celebration. But he said to his father, 'All these years I've worked hard for you and never once refused to do what you asked me to do. You never even killed a goat for me so my friends and I could have a party. But as soon as this, your son, comes back home after squandering your money on prostitutes and luxurious living, you kill the best calf and have a party for him!'

"The father replied, 'Son, the whole farm and everything I have is yours. You and I have always been close. It's the right thing to do to celebrate your brother's return. I thought he was dead, but he's alive! He was lost but is found!'" (Luke 15).

Foresight

Jesus continued, "A certain rich man had a manager who was accused of fraud and waste. So the man called him in and said, 'What's this I hear about your mismanaging my money? I'll have this checked out, and if it proves true, I'll have to let you go.'

"The manager said to himself, 'I know I'll lose my job. So what am I going to do? I'm not strong enough to dig ditches, and I'm too embarrassed to beg. I know what I'll do! I'll obligate people to me so that when I'm dismissed, I'll have lots of friends to help me out.'

"So he asked each one who owed his master money to visit him. He asked the first one, 'How much do you owe?'

"The man answered, 'Eight hundred gallons of olive oil.'

"The manager said, 'Let me see the bill. I'll change it to read 400.'

"The next one came, and the manager asked, 'How much do you owe?'

"The man answered, 'A thousand bushels of wheat.'

"The manager said, 'Let me see the bill. I'll change it to read 800.'

"When the rich man heard about it, he commended the dishonest manager for his shrewdness and foresight. The unbelievers of this world give more thought to their future than the people of light.

"He who is faithful in little things will be faithful in big things. He who is dishonest in little things will be dishonest in big things. If you can't be trusted with earthly riches, how can you be trusted with spiritual riches? If you can't be trusted handling other people's money, who will want to hire you?

"You can't serve two masters. You'll have to choose one or the other. If not, you'll eventually end up hating one and loving the other, or vice versa. You can't serve God and money."

This really bothered the Pharisees, because they loved money and thought that being rich showed they had God's favor. So they ridiculed Jesus not only for what He said, but also because He was poor.

Jesus responded, "You're very skilled at making yourself look good in front of people, but God knows your heart. What people do to make themselves look important is not pleasing to God.

"The laws of Moses and the writings of the prophets were the only guides the people had until John the Baptist came. Since then the kingdom of God is being plainly preached, and people are responding and pressing to come in. But that doesn't mean what has been written has lost its force. It's easier for heaven and earth to pass away than for the smallest letter to be deleted from the law.

"A case in point is marriage. Anyone who divorces his wife over some triviality so he can marry someone else is committing adultery. And anyone who sees this as an opportunity to marry this divorced woman is committing adultery" (Luke 16:1-18).

Selfishness

Then Jesus came back to His original point about caring for others and said, "You tell the story of a certain rich man who loved to dress in the best clothes, live in luxury, and feast every day. At his gate sat a poor man named Lazarus, who was hungry and longed for the scraps that fell from the rich man's table. The neighborhood dogs would come and lick his sores. Finally the poor man died, and, as you tell the story, he was carried by angels to sit next to Abraham.

"Soon the rich man also died and was taken to the place of the dead, where he was in torment. As he looked up, he saw Lazarus sitting next to Abraham. So he called out, 'Father Abraham, have mercy on me and send Lazarus here with a little water to cool my tongue, because I'm suffering terribly.'

"Abraham said, 'Son, remember how luxuriously you lived and how poor Lazarus was? You had everything, and he had nothing. Now he's happy and sitting next to me, while you're suffering. Besides, there is a fixed chasm between here and there so that no one from here can go there and no one from there can come here.'

"The rich man responded, 'I beg you, then, to send Lazarus to my father's house, for I have five brothers who need to be warned so that they don't end up here.'

"Abraham replied, 'They have Moses and the prophets—let them listen to them.'

"The rich man answered, 'No, Father Abraham, but if someone from the dead would go and speak to them, they would listen.'

"Abraham said, 'If they won't listen to Moses and the prophets, they won't be convinced if someone rises from the dead'" (Luke 19:19-31).

Forgiveness and Faith

Then Jesus turned back to His disciples and said, "People will always be tempted, but how terrible it will be for those who deliberately tempt and lead others into sin. It would be better for those people to have a stone tied around their necks and be thrown into the sea than to draw others, especially those newly come to the faith, away from God. So be careful what you do. If a fellow believer sins against you, say something to him about it, and if he repents, forgive him. If he wrongs you seven times in one day and says he's sorry, forgive him."

One of the disciples asked, "Master, how do we get more faith?"

Jesus answered, "It's not how much faith you have, but if you have the right kind. Even if that faith were the size of a tiny mustard seed, you could say to this mulberry tree, 'Pull yourself up by the roots and plant yourself in the sea,' and if God wanted it to happen, it would.

"But consider this instead: When a servant who has sold himself to someone to pay off his debt comes in from plowing the field or taking care of the sheep, does he sit down to eat? Wouldn't the master say, 'Wash up and put on an apron and get supper ready. When you're done, you may sit down and eat too'? Will he praise his servant for doing what he was expected to do? In the same way, if you do what you were asked to do, you should say to yourselves, 'We don't deserve any special praise, because we simply did what was expected of us'" (Luke 17:1-10).

eighteen

Divine Power

Now about this time a friend of Jesus named Lazarus, the brother of Mary and Martha, was very sick. (This was the Mary who later poured expensive perfume on Jesus' feet at Simon's house and wiped them with her long hair.) The sisters lived in Bethany, not far from Jerusalem. They sent word to Jesus that His friend Lazarus was sick.

When Jesus heard that Lazarus was sick, He said, "His sickness will not end in death, but it will glorify God, and through it the Son of Man will also receive glory." Although Jesus loved the family, He remained in the same place for two more days. The following morning He said to His disciples, "Let's go back to Judea."

The disciples objected, "Lord, we were just down in Judea, and the Jewish leaders wanted to stone You to death. Are You sure You want to go back there?"

Jesus answered, "There are 12 hours of daylight, during which people do their work. At night you can't get much done because it's dark." Then he added, "Our friend Lazarus is sound asleep. I need to go and wake him up."

The disciples responded, "If he's having a good sleep, that means he's getting better."

But Jesus was talking about death. They thought He was talking about a good night's rest. Jesus then made it plain by stating, "Lazarus is dead. I'm glad I wasn't there when he was sick, because what will happen next will increase your faith in Me. So come—let's go."

Thomas said to the others, "Come, let's go—we might as well die with Him."

By the time Jesus got to Judea, Lazarus had already been dead for four days. Bethany was only about two miles from Jerusalem. Many of the people who knew the family had come to pay their respects and comfort Mary and Martha. As soon as Martha got word that Jesus was nearing Bethany, she slipped out of the house and went to meet Him. Mary didn't notice that her sister had left, so she stayed in the house, crying.

When Martha saw Jesus, she rushed up to Him and said, "Lord, if only You had been here, my brother would not have died, because I know that whatever You ask God to do, He does it."

Jesus replied, "Don't worry—your brother will live again."

Martha said, "I know that he'll live again with all the others who will be resurrected in the last day."

Jesus looked at her sympathetically and said, "I am the resurrection and the life. Those who believe in Me, even though they die, will live and never die again. Do you believe this?"

Martha answered, "Yes, Lord, I believe that You are the Messiah, the Son of the living God, who has come here to save us."

Then she turned and went to get Mary. She slipped into the house, called Mary to one side, and whispered, "The Master is here and wants to see you." Quickly they both left to see Jesus, who had stayed outside the village, where Martha had met Him earlier. When the people in the house saw the two sisters leave, they said to each other, "They're probably going to the gravesite. Let's go along." But the sisters went to see Jesus, and when Mary saw Him, she rushed up to Him, fell at His feet, and said, "Lord, if only You had been here, my brother would not have died!"

When Jesus saw Mary on her knees crying, and the people who had come with her crying, He groaned and asked, "Where did you bury him?"

They said, "Come—we'll show you." Then Jesus cried also. The people closest to Him said, "Look, He's crying. He must have loved him very much." Others said, "If He loved him that much, why didn't He come and heal him? He even healed a man born blind. He could have healed Lazarus and kept him from dying."

When Jesus came to the tomb, he groaned and cried again. Then He said to the men nearby, "Roll away the stone from the entrance."

Martha spoke up, "Lord, the smell will be terrible, because he's been dead for four days!" Jesus turned to her and said, "Didn't I tell you that if you would believe, you would see the power of God?"

After the men rolled away the stone, Jesus looked up to heaven and said loud enough for all to hear, "Father, thank You for hearing Me. I know that You always hear Me, but I'm saying this so that the people will believe that You sent Me."

Then Jesus looked at the entrance of the tomb and with a loud voice commanded, "Lazarus, come out!" And Lazarus appeared at the entrance, still wrapped in his burial clothes. Jesus said to the men, "Unwrap him!"

When the people at the gravesite saw this happen, many believed that

Jesus was the Messiah, including some of the Jewish leaders from Jerusalem (John 11:1-45).

Plot to Kill Jesus

Some at the gravesite with Mary and Martha who saw Lazarus resurrected rushed back to Jerusalem to tell the Pharisees what had happened. So the leading Pharisees and chief priests called a council meeting to decide what to do. They said to each other, "What are we going to do? This man Jesus is performing some unheard-of miracles. Soon the whole country will follow Him and make Him king. Then the Romans will come, destroy our Temple, and dissolve our nation."

Then Caiaphas, the high priest, said, "You're overlooking one thing. Why should we let our nation be dissolved for the sake of one man? Let Him die to save the country." Without knowing it, he had stated a prophecy. Jesus would die to save not only Israel but God's people everywhere.

From that time on they began to plot to put Jesus to death. So He stopped His public ministry in Jerusalem or Judea and went with His disciples to a village called Ephraim, near the wilderness, and stayed there.

Soon it was time for the Passover, and people from all over the country went to Jerusalem a few days early to purify themselves. Many of them went to the Temple looking for Jesus. They asked each other, "Do you think He'll come or not?" They said this because the leading priests and Pharisees had announced that if anyone saw Jesus or knew where He was, they should let them know so they could arrest Him (John 11:46-57).

Ten Lepers

As Jesus made His way south to Jerusalem for the Passover, He passed along the borders of Samaria and Galilee. As He approached a certain village, 10 lepers came out to meet Him. They stood at a distance and called out to Him, "Master, have mercy on us!" Jesus turned to them and said, "First go and show yourselves to the priest as required by law." They did what He asked, and on the way they were healed.

One of them, when he saw that he was healed, ran back to Jesus, praising God as loudly as he could. He fell on the ground at Jesus' feet, thanking Him for what He had done. The man was not a Jew, but a Samaritan.

Jesus asked him, "Didn't I heal 10 lepers? Where are the other nine? Are you the only one who came back to thank Me and give glory to God? Come, stand up and then be on your way. Your faith in Me has made you well" (Luke 17:11-19).

At one time some of the Pharisees asked Jesus, "When will the kingdom of God come?"

He answered, "The kingdom of God will not come the way you think. You won't be able to point to it and say, 'Here it is!' or 'There it is!' because the kingdom of God is right in front of you."

Later Jesus talked about the kingdom of God with His disciples and said, "The time is coming when you will look back on these days and long for Me to be here again, but it won't happen. Reports that people saw Me over here or over there will reach you, but don't believe it and go looking for Me. My coming will be like lightning in the sky. Everyone will see it. But before then the Son of Man will be arrested and rejected by His own people.

"Just before I come back, things will be like they were in the days of Noah before the Flood. The people were engrossed in eating, drinking, and marrying as often as they wished, right up to the day that Noah and his family went into the ark and the Flood came and swept them all away.

"Also, it will be like it was in the days of Lot. People were caught up in eating, drinking, buying, selling, farming, and building, right up to the day that Lot was guided out of Sodom and fire came down from heaven and destroyed them all. That's how it will be in the time of the end just before the Son of Man comes back.

"In those days people relaxing on the roofs of their houses shouldn't be so concerned about their belongings. And those in the field shouldn't be concerned about the farm. Remember what happened to Lot's wife, whose heart was still on what she had in Sodom. Whoever clings to life in this world will lose it, and whoever is willing to give up this life will save it.

"Of two people in the same bed—one will be saved and the other will not. Of two people on the same job—one will be saved and the other will not."

Then the disciples asked Jesus, "When will all this take place?"

He answered, "When people see a group of vultures waiting in a tree, they know that down below a life is ending. So when people see the signs I just talked about, they will know that the end is near" (Luke 17:20-37).

Story of a Judge

Then Jesus told His disciples a story about the importance of persistent prayer: "In a certain city there was a judge who had no respect for the things of God and didn't care about others—only himself. In the same town there was a widow who went to the judge repeatedly, pleading with him to give her some legal protection against her opponent in a legal case. For a long time the judge ignored her, but eventually he said to himself, 'This woman is wearing me out. Even though I'm not afraid of God or man, I'm going to settle this case and see that justice is done.'"

Jesus asked, "Did you notice what the judge said? Even this wicked judge finally did what was right for the woman. Don't you think that God will do what is right for His people who plead with Him for justice? He will not forget them, but when the time comes, He will do it quickly. However, the more important question is: When I come back, how many people will I find who really have faith in Me?" (Luke 18:1-8).

Two Different Men

Next Jesus told a story to some who thought they were righteous but despised others. "Two men went to the Temple to pray. One was a Pharisee and the other a tax collector. The Pharisee walked to the front and prayed, 'God, I'm thankful that I'm not like others who are downright evil, defrauding people and living in adultery, or like this tax collector who takes our money and gives it to the Romans. I fast twice a week, pay my tithe, and come daily to the Temple.'

"The tax collector stood in the back and didn't even look up, but clutched his chest and prayed, 'O God, be merciful to me, a sinner.' The tax collector went home forgiven, but not the Pharisee. Those who exalt themselves will be humbled, but those who sense their need and humble themselves will be exalted" (Luke 18:9-14).

nineteen

Tricky Questions

When Jesus left Galilee, He headed toward Judea from east of the Jordan River. Great crowds followed Him, and He healed all their sick. Some of the Pharisees came to Him and decided to trap Him with this question: "Is it right for a man to divorce his wife and marry someone else for any reason he comes up with?"

Jesus answered, "Haven't you read the Scriptures? In the beginning God made them male and female and blessed them. That's why a man leaves his father and mother and gets married and the two become one. So they are no longer two, but one. Let no one pull them apart. That is not what God had in mind."

They asked a second question: "Then why did Moses say it's permissible to get divorced as long as it's done legally and put in writing?"

Jesus answered, "Moses did this to stop men from treating their wives so wickedly by just setting them aside. A man who divorces his wife, except for adultery, and then marries another is committing adultery. The same applies to a woman. If she divorces her husband over some triviality and then marries another, she's also committing adultery."

The disciples exclaimed, "If that's the case, it's better not to get married!"

Jesus responded, "Not everyone can live a married life—only those who have the aptitude for it. Some never give marriage a second thought. They just weren't born for it. Others don't marry because of circumstances. And still others choose to stay single to advance God's kingdom. But those who really want to get married should get married" (Matt. 19:1-12).

Children

After Jesus stopped teaching, mothers crowded in with their little ones to have Him pray for their children and bless them. The disciples told the mothers to go away and not bother Him. When Jesus saw what was happening, He said to His disciples, "Don't stop them. Let the children come to Me.

This kind of faith and love is what the kingdom of heaven is all about." Then He took the little ones in His arms, prayed for them, and blessed them. When He was done, He continued on his way to Jerusalem (Matt. 19:13-15).

A Wealthy Young Man

Along the way a young man came to Jesus and asked Him, "Good and righteous Teacher, what good things should I do to make sure of eternal life?"

Jesus answered, "Why would you call Me good and righteous? God is the only one who is righteous and good. If you want to make sure of heaven, keep the commandments. You know them: Don't kill. Don't commit adultery. Don't steal. Don't lie. Honor your father and mother. And care about your neighbor as you care about yourself."

The young man said, "Teacher, I've kept the commandments since I was a child. What else should I do?"

Jesus felt genuine love for this young man and answered, "There's one more thing you need to do. Go, sell all you have, give the money to the poor, then come and follow Me, and you'll have treasure waiting for you in heaven." When the young man heard this, he became very sad and turned and walked away, because he was extremely wealthy.

Then Jesus said to His disciples, "It's hard for wealthy people to make it to heaven. In fact, it's easier for a camel to go through the eye of a needle than for a rich man to depend on God and be saved."

The disciples were shocked. They believed the wealthy were rich because God had blessed them. So they said, "If the rich can't be saved, who can?"

Jesus said, "To you it might seem impossible, but with God everything is possible."

Then Peter spoke up, "Lord, what about us? We've left everything to follow You!"

Jesus answered, "The truth is that when I come back and sit on My throne, you also will sit on thrones helping to judge Israel. Everyone who has for My sake given up houses and lands, or left father, mother, brothers, sisters, wife, or children, will receive much more—and eternal life. Many who are first now will end up last or not be there, and many who are last now will be the first ones to be saved" (Matt. 19:16-30).

Wages

Jesus continued: "The question of who will enter the kingdom of God reminds Me of the owner of a huge vineyard who needed workers to harvest his grapes. At six o'clock in the morning he went to the marketplace, where men wait for work. He offered to pay them a normal wage for a day's work, and they agreed. At nine o'clock he went back to the marketplace for more workers. He offered to pay them whatever was right, and they agreed. Soon he needed still more workers. So at noon he went back to the marketplace, and again at three o'clock.

"At five o'clock he realized he had to have more workers to finish the harvest before dark. So again he went to the marketplace and saw some men standing around looking for work. He asked them, 'Have you been waiting for work all day?' They answered, 'Yes, but no one has hired us.' He said, 'Come, work in my vineyard, and I'll pay you what's right.'

"When evening came and the harvest was done, the vineyard owner told his foreman to call the men together and pay them, beginning with the last ones hired. So the workers who were hired at five o'clock lined up first and got a full day's pay. When the others saw this, they assumed they would get more. But they all got a full day's pay.

"Then some of them protested, 'Those who came to work at five o'clock worked only one hour. How can they get the same pay when we worked all day in scorching heat?'

"The vineyard owner said to one of them, 'Friend, I haven't been unfair. Didn't you agree to work for a full day's pay? Collect your wages, be thankful, and go home to your family. If I want to pay those hired last the same as those hired first, is that wrong? Can't I do what I want with my own money? Are you angry because I'm being generous?'

"That's how it will be when God's harvest ends. Many who were hired first will be last, and many who were hired last will be first" (Matt. 20:1-16).

Jesus Predicts His Death

As they continued on their way, Jesus walked ahead of them, eager to get to Jerusalem. His disciples were amazed, and the people who followed were afraid. Once when Jesus stopped to rest, He took His disciples aside and said, "When we get to Jerusalem, the Son of Man will be arrested and handed over to the chief priests and experts in religious law. They will hand down the death sentence and turn Him over to the Romans, who will mock Him, spit on Him, scourge Him unmercifully, and then crucify Him. But on the third day He will rise again" (Matt. 20:17-19; Mark 10:32-34).

Greatness

As they neared Jericho, the mother of James and John came with her sons to Jesus, knelt down, and asked if He would grant her a favor.

He said, "What is it?"

She answered, "Lord, when You set up Your kingdom, would You let my two sons sit next to You, one on the right and the other on the left?" Then James and John spoke up and asked for the same favor.

Jesus answered, "You don't understand what you're asking. Are you able to drink the cup of suffering I must drink, and the pain with which I must be baptized?"

They responded, "Yes, Lord, we're able!"

Jesus said, "Yes, you will drink from the same cup and be baptized with the baptism, but I can't say who will sit next to Me in my kingdom. That's the Father's decision."

When the other 10 disciples heard what the two brothers and their mother had asked Jesus, they became angry.

Jesus called them together and said, "You know that in this world, rulers lord their authority over people, and those in high places misuse their influence. But that's not the way it should be among you. Whoever wants to be great must be willing to serve, and whoever wants to be first must be willing to be last. Even the Son of Man did not come to be served, but to serve, and to give his life as a ransom to free many" (Matt. 20:20-28; Mark 10:32-45).

Up a Tree

When Jesus and His disciples came to Jericho and were making their way through town, a wealthy Jew named Zacchaeus, who collected taxes from his people for the Romans, wanted to see Jesus. But he was very short and couldn't see over the heads of the people. So he ran ahead and climbed up into a sycamore tree to get a good look at Jesus, who was coming down the road. Jesus stopped under the sycamore tree, looked up, and said, "Zacchaeus, hurry down. I must stop at your house and talk to you today."

Zacchaeus couldn't believe it! Excited, he quickly climbed down and led the way to his house. When the people saw the two of them walking together, they complained. "Look!" they said, "He's going to the house of a tax collector and sinner!"

Once inside, Jesus talked about the kingdom of God. Suddenly Zacchaeus stood up and said, "I'll give half of what I own to the poor, and to those I've overcharged on taxes I'll give back four times as much!"

Jesus responded, "Today salvation has come to your house. You are a true son of Abraham. The Son of Man has come to seek and to save all who are lost" (Luke 19:1-10).

All this time the people were listening to everything that Jesus said. He knew what was in their hearts. So he told them a story to correct the idea they had that He would set up His kingdom as soon as He got to Jerusalem.

He said to them, "A young man of noble birth was called to a distant country to be crowned king, and then he would come back. Before leaving, he called together 10 servants and gave each a certain sum of money to manage for him while he was gone. But his people hated him and sent a delegation after him to let it be known that they didn't want him to be their king.

"When he returned, he called together his 10 servants and wanted to know what they had done with his money. The first servant said, 'Your Majesty, here is 10 times the money you gave me.'

"The king replied, 'Well done! You're a good servant. Because I could trust you with what I gave you, I'm putting you in charge of 10 of my cities.'

"Then the second servant came up and said, 'Your Majesty, here is five times the money you gave me.'

"The king answered, 'Well done! You're a good servant. I can depend on you to be faithful with what I gave you, so I'm putting you in charge of five of my cities.'

"Another servant came up and said, 'Your Majesty, I was afraid of what you might say if I didn't do well with what you gave me. I know you expect a lot, so I thought it best to hide your money and keep it in a safe place. Here it is.'

"The king replied, 'You did not do well. The least you could have done was to put my money in the bank for others to use and have it draw interest.' Then the king turned to his attendants and said, 'Take back the money I gave him and give it to the one who did the best.'

"The attendants replied, 'But, your Majesty, he already has enough.'

"The king declared, 'Everyone who is trustworthy will be given more, and those on whom I can't depend will lose what I gave them.'

"Then the king ordered the guards to bring in those who didn't want him to be king. When they came in, he ordered them executed in his presence."

After Jesus told this story, He left Jericho and continued on His way to Jerusalem (Luke 19:11-28).

A Blind Man

At the outskirts of Jericho, a blind beggar named Bartimaeus sat by the side of the road. When someone told him that Jesus was coming by, he began to shout, "Jesus, Son of David, have mercy on me!" People tried to quiet him, but he shouted that much louder, "Son of David! Have mercy on me!"

When Jesus got to where Bartimaeus sat, He stopped and said to those nearby, "Tell him to come over here."

The people called to him, "Bartimaeus, Jesus wants to see you! Get up. Come, we'll guide you."

Bartimaeus threw aside his covering, jumped up, and was introduced to Jesus. Jesus asked him, "What do you want Me to do for you?"

Bartimaeus answered, "Master, I want to see again!"

Jesus looked at him intently and said, "Your faith in Me has made you well. Be on your way."

Instantly Bartimaeus could see, and he joined the crowd following Jesus down the road toward Jerusalem (Mark 10:46-52).

twenty

Invitation to Dinner

Six days before the Passover, Jesus arrived in Bethany, which was not far from Jerusalem. He stopped there to see His friend Lazarus, whom He had raised from the dead, and Lazarus' two sisters, Mary and Martha.

While He was in town, Simon the Pharisee, whom Jesus had healed of leprosy, invited Him and His disciples and friends to dinner. Jesus was the honored guest, and Lazarus sat next to Him and Martha served. That was when Mary took a 12-ounce jar of expensive perfumed oil, quietly slipped over to where Jesus sat, and anointed His feet with it. Then she wiped His feet dry with her long hair. The fragrance filled the house.

Judas Iscariot, one of the disciples, said loudly, "What a waste! This perfumed oil could have been sold and the money given to the poor!" He said that not because he cared for the poor, but because he was treasurer of the group and had been using some of the money for himself.

Jesus quietly said to Judas, "Leave the woman alone. She's anointing My body for burial. There will always be poor people who need help. But I won't be here much longer" (John 12:1-8). "Wherever this gospel is preached around the world, what she has done for Me will also be told" (Mark 14:9).

Simon thought to himself, "How can this man be the long-expected Prophet, our Messiah? If He were, He would know what kind of woman this is. He wouldn't let her touch Him." Jesus knew what he was thinking. He turned and said, "Simon, let Me tell you a story, and I would like to know what you think of it. There were two people who owed a rich man some money. One owed him 500 silver coins, and the other 50. When neither one could pay his debt, the man forgave them both. Which one of these men would be more appreciative?"

Simon answered, "The one who had the more forgiven."

Jesus said, "You're right."

He turned toward the woman and said to Simon, "Did you notice how thoughtful she has been? When I came to your house, no one offered Me a basin of water and a towel to rinse the dust off My feet, as is customary. But this woman has washed My feet with her tears and wiped them with her hair. You didn't give Me the ancient kiss of welcome or put oil on My head, but she has anointed My feet with perfumed oil. Though her sins are many, they've been forgiven, and she's extremely grateful. Those who think they have only a few minor sins show little gratitude for forgiveness."

Jesus said to the woman, "Your sins are forgiven."

When those at the table heard this, they whispered to each other, "How can He forgive sins? Only God can do that."

Then Jesus said to the woman so that everyone could hear, "Your faith in Me has saved you. Go in peace" (Luke 7:36-50).

The Plot to Kill

Many people had heard of Jesus' arrival in Bethany and had flocked to see Him and Lazarus, whom He had raised from the dead. But the leading priests were making plans to kill both Jesus and Lazarus. It was because of Lazarus that so many people believed that Jesus was the Messiah (John 12:9-11).

Then Judas went to the chief priests and asked, "What will you pay me if I tell you where you can arrest Jesus without causing a disturbance?" They offered him 30 pieces of silver (the price of a slave), which he accepted. From that time on Judas watched for the right moment to turn Him over to the priests (Matt. 26:14-16).

Two days later it was time for the Passover, followed by the weeklong Festival of Unleavened Bread. The chief priests and experts of the law were trying to figure out how to execute Jesus without causing a riot. They said to each other, "When we do it, let's not do it during Passover week, or the people might rise up to defend Him" (Mark 14:1, 2).

Jerusalem

As Jesus and His disciples neared Jerusalem, they stopped at the little village of Bethphage on the Mount of Olives. Jesus said to two of His disciples, "Go into the village, and right by the entrance you'll see a donkey tied to a post with a young colt by her side. Untie them and bring them here. If anyone stops you and asks what you're doing, just say, 'The Lord needs them.' Then he'll let you take them."

This was according to the prophecy of Zechariah, which said, "Tell the people of Israel, 'Look! Your King is coming! He's humble, just riding on a donkey, even the young colt of a lowly working animal.' "

The two disciples went and found the mother and her colt at the entrance of the town just as Jesus had said. As they were untying them, the owner came out and asked, "What are you doing?"

They answered, "The Lord needs them."

The owner agreed, so they took the donkeys to Jesus. He chose to ride on the colt, which no one had ever ridden. So they threw their cloaks over the young colt, and Jesus got on.

When the people saw this, they quickly caught the meaning and spread their cloaks on the road ahead of Jesus. Others cut off palm branches and spread them on the road. Then they started shouting, "Praise God for the Son of David! He will save us! Our King is coming! He is coming in the name of the Lord! Glory to God in the highest!" (Matt. 21:1-9).

Some of the Pharisees in the crowd yelled, "Teacher! Stop them! Can't You hear what they're saying?"

Jesus called back, "If I stop them, the stones along the road will cry out."

As they came down the Mount of Olives, Jesus looked at the city and began to cry. Through His tears he said, "O Jerusalem, if you only knew, even as late as today, what you need to bring in peace. But you are so blind. Soon the time will come when your enemies will surround you, build ramparts against your walls, and close in on you from all sides. They will level you to the ground and kill your children. They will not leave one stone unturned—all because you didn't recognize the day when God came to visit you" (Luke 19:39-44).

When the procession reached the Temple, Jesus got off the colt. Then He went into the Temple and saw the courtyard filled with merchants buying and selling sheep and doves for sacrifice and exchanging money for Temple coins. He was so hurt by the desecration of God's house that He turned over the tables of the money changers, untied the sheep, opened the cages of the doves, and said in a commanding voice: "The Scripture is clear: 'My house shall be a house of prayer, not a marketplace.' But you have turned it into a den of thieves!"

Then quiet settled over the Temple and the lame and the blind came in to see Jesus. He healed them all and blessed them.

When the leading priests and the experts of the law saw the lame and the blind being healed and heard the children chanting, "Hosanna to the Son of David," they were really upset. They went over to Jesus and complained, "Can't You hear what these children are saying about You?"

Jesus answered, "Haven't you read what it says in the Psalms: 'Out of the mouth of children will come praise'?"

Then He left the Temple and went back to Bethany to stay overnight (Matt. 21:12-17).

Confrontation

The next morning before breakfast Jesus and His disciples made their way back to Jerusalem. On the way He saw a fig tree beside the road. To satisfy His hunger, He went over to find some figs, but the tree had only lush-looking leaves—no fruit. He decided to use the tree as an object lesson. So He said to the tree, "You will never produce fruit again!" Immediately the leaves began to shrivel up.

In amazement the disciples exclaimed, "Look! The leaves are curling up!"

Jesus said, "Don't be so surprised. If you have faith, you'll not only be able to do what I just did, but you could say to this nearby mountain, 'Out of my way and throw yourself into the sea,' and if it is God's will, it will happen. If you pray and believe, you will be amazed what God will do to help you" (Matt. 21:18-22).

Soon Jesus and His disciples arrived in Jerusalem and made their way to the Temple. The leading priests, elders, and experts in the law were waiting for Him. They said, "Who gave You the authority to do what You did yesterday?"

Jesus answered, "Let me ask you a question first—then I'll answer yours. By whose authority did John preach and baptize? By God's, or his own?"

They got into a huddle and said to each other, "If we say under God's authority, He'll say, 'Then why didn't you do what he said?' If we say he did it on his own authority, the people will turn against us, because they believe that John was a prophet." So they turned back to Jesus and admitted, "We can't answer Your question."

Jesus replied, "That means I don't have to answer your question and tell you by what authority I do things" (Mark 11:27-33).

Jesus Makes His Point

"Let Me ask you a different question," Jesus continued. "What do you think of this? A man had two sons and said to the firstborn, 'Son, could you go and work in the vineyard to help with the harvest?'

"The son answered, 'No, I am not going!' But as he thought about it, he changed his mind and went.

"Then the father asked the other son, 'Son, could you go and work in the vineyard to help with the harvest?'

"This son answered, 'Sure, Father.' But he never went. Which son obeyed the father?"

The priests answered, "The first one, of course."

Jesus replied, "You're right. That's why tax collectors and prostitutes will be let into the kingdom before you. They listened to John and changed their ways, but you didn't" (Matt. 21:28-32).

"Or what do you think of this? A certain landowner planted a vineyard, built a wall around it, dug a place for the winepress, and put up a watchtower to spot thieves. Then he leased the vineyard to grape growers and left the country on business. At harvesttime he returned home and sent one of his servants to collect his percentage of the profits. But the vineyard keepers beat the servant up and sent him back empty-handed. The landowner sent another servant, but they threw rocks at him, struck him in the head, shamed him publicly, and sent him back. When the landowner sent a third servant, they killed him. Others who were sent were either beaten or killed.

"Then the landowner decided to send his son, the only one he had. He said to himself, 'I'm sure they'll respect my son.' But when the vineyard keepers saw the son coming, they said to each other, 'He's the heir. Let's kill him. Then we can claim the vineyard!' So that's what they did. They took hold of the son, killed him, and threw his body out of the vineyard.

"What do you think the landowner will do to those tenants? Let me tell you. He'll come and have them arrested and tried for murder. Then he'll lease the vineyard to others. That's what it means when the scripture says, 'The stone which the Temple builders rejected was the very one they needed for the cornerstone.' Don't be surprised at what God can do."

When the leading priests and experts in the law heard this, they knew He was talking about them. They wanted to capture Him, but were afraid because the people believed Jesus to be a prophet. So they turned away and left (Mark 12:1-12).

twenty one

Jesus' Final Week of Teaching

The Wedding

Jesus taught the people by stories. He said, "The kingdom of heaven is like what happened to a king who prepared a wedding feast for his son. Many guests were invited, and when everything was ready, he sent his servants to remind everyone that it was time to come. But no one did. So he sent other servants to tell them, 'The banquet is ready. The choicest meats of lamb and veal and all kinds of special delicacies are waiting for you. Come, hurry!' But they ignored the servants and went about life as usual, one to his farm and another to his business. Others beat the servants, mistreated them, and even killed some of them.

"When the king heard about this, he was deeply hurt. So he sent his troops to destroy those who had murdered his servants and to burn their city. Then he said to his servants, 'The wedding is ready, and those who were invited didn't come. They're not worthy to be here. So go out into the highways and invite all those you see to come to the wedding.' The king's servants went out and brought in all they could find, good and bad alike, and the banquet hall was filled with guests. Then the king came in to welcome the guests. He saw a man who wasn't wearing the clothes the king had provided for those who attended the wedding. He said to him, 'Friend, how come you're wearing your own clothes and not the wedding garment?'

"The man had no excuse. So he just stood there and said nothing.

"Then the king said to his servants, 'Take him, tie him up, and throw him outside, where it's dark. There will be weeping and gnashing of teeth.'

"Many are called, but few are chosen to stay" (Matt. 22:1-14).

Taxes

Then the Pharisees met together and decided to try to get Jesus to say something that they could use as an excuse to arrest Him. So they sent some of their brightest young members, together with the supporters of Herod, to trip Him up.

They said, "Teacher, we know that You're an honest man, and that You teach what is right and show people the way of God without favoring anyone, no matter who they are. So let us ask You, Is it right for us to pay taxes to the Roman government?"

Jesus replied, "You hypocrites! Why are you asking this question so innocently and then trying to trap Me with it? Let me see a Roman coin."

When they showed Him one, he asked, "Whose picture and title is on it?"

They answered, "Caesar's."

He said, "Give to Caesar what belongs to him, and to God what belongs to Him." They were so surprised at His simple answer that they turned and walked away (Matt. 22:15-22).

Marriage in Heaven

Later that same day the Sadducees, who say there is no resurrection, asked Jesus, "Teacher, Moses said that if a man dies and he and his wife had no children, his brother should marry her to leave an heir for his dead brother. Now, we know a case in which there were seven brothers. The first one got married and soon died, but left no children, and left his wife to his brother. The same thing happened to the second and the third, until all seven had married her. Finally the woman died. So tell us, whose wife will she be when she gets to heaven? She had been married to all seven!"

Jesus answered, "You've deceived yourselves with your own reasoning. There will be a resurrection, but there will be no marriages or giving in marriage, because God's people will be like the angels in heaven. Haven't you read in Scripture where God says, 'I am the God of Abraham, Isaac, and Jacob'? This means that God is not the God of the dead, but of the living, because through His power Isaac was born."

When the people heard this, they were amazed at Jesus' simple answers to hard questions (Matt. 22:23-33).

Jesus and the Lawyer

When the Pharisees heard that the Sadducees had not succeeded, they decided to send a lawyer, an expert in religious law, to trip up Jesus. He asked, "Teacher, which one of the commandments is the most important?"

Jesus answered, "According to Scripture, the most important commandment is: 'Hear, O Israel, the Lord our God is the only Lord. You should love the Lord your God with all your heart, all your soul, all your mind, and all your strength.' And the second is just as important: 'You should love and care about your neighbor as you do yourself.' No other commandments are as important as these two."

The lawyer complimented Jesus: "Well said! There is only one God, and we should love and serve Him with all our hearts, our understanding, our souls, and our strength, and also love and care about our neighbor. This is more important than all the sacrifices and burnt offerings we can bring."

Jesus responded, "Good! You're not far from the kingdom."

After this, they gave up trying to trap Jesus (Matt. 22:34-40; Mark 12:28-34).

A Tough Question

Then Jesus said to the Pharisees, "Let Me ask you a question: What do you think of the Messiah? Whose descendant will He be?"

They answered, "The son of David, of course."

Jesus responded, "Then why does David, speaking under the inspiration of the Holy Spirit, call Him 'Lord' when he says, 'The God of Israel said to my Lord, Come, sit at My right hand until I subdue your enemies and bring them to your feet'? If David called the Messiah 'Lord,' how can He also be his Son?"

The Pharisees couldn't answer the question. So they never challenged Jesus again (Matt. 22:41-46).

Seven Warnings

Then turning back to His critics, Jesus said, "Woe to you, Pharisees and experts in the law. Hypocrites! You keep people out of heaven and aren't fit to go in yourselves. You put on a big show with long prayers, and then turn around and rob widows of their property to enrich yourselves.

"Woe to you, Pharisees and experts in the law! You travel land and sea to make one convert, but then turn him into twice as much a product of hell as you.

"Woe to you, blind guides, who say to the people, 'An oath doesn't mean anything if taken in the name of the Temple—only if you take it by the gold of the Temple'! Fools! Which has greater value, the gold or the Temple itself? Also you tell them, 'An oath taken in the name of the altar doesn't mean anything—only if you take it by the sacrifices put on it.' Fools! Which is more important, the sacrifices and offerings, or what the altar stands for? An oath taken in the name of the altar includes everything on it, and an oath taken in the name of the Temple includes the name of God, whose house it is.

"Woe to you, Pharisees and experts in the law! How ignorant can you be! You are so careful to tithe the least income, even what you get from spices in your garden, but overlook what's most important, such as fairness, kindness, and faith. You should tithe, but not forget the other. How blind can you be! You filter your water to strain out any gnats that might be in it, and then end up swallowing a camel.

"Woe to you, Pharisees and experts in the law! You are so careful to wash your cups and dishes, but your hands are unclean and dirty.

"Woe to you, Pharisees and experts in the law! Hypocrites! You're like beautiful tombstones—nice on the outside but full of dead bones underneath. You appear so holy, but you're full of hypocrisy and disobedience.

"Woe to you, Pharisees and experts in the law! Hypocrites! You build monuments to honor the prophets and say, 'If we had lived back when our ancestors did, we would not have killed the prophets as they did.' By saying this, you're admitting that God's people could do the same today. Go ahead! Fill up the cup of rebellion that your ancestors started. I know you're planning to kill Me. You're as slippery as snakes. How do you expect to escape the judgment that will condemn you to extinction in hell?

"I will send you prophets, wise men, and teachers, some of whom you will kill and crucify, and others you will scourge in your synagogues and persecute from city to city. You will reap the consequences of accumulated guilt from the murder of righteous Abel down to the murder of the prophet Zechariah by the altar in the Temple. All this will come on you in this generation."

Jesus Grieves Over Jerusalem

"O Jerusalem, Jerusalem, the city that kills the prophets and stones God's messengers! How many times I wanted to gather your people and protect them, as a hen gathers her chicks under her wings to protect them, but you were not willing! So now your city is left desolate and without protection. You refuse to acknowledge Me until you see Me come again. Then you will say, 'Blessings and praise! He is coming in the name of the Lord!' But it will be too late" (Matt. 23:13-39; Mark 12:38-40).

The Widow

As Jesus was teaching in the Temple, He went to sit near the offering box so that He could watch people putting in their offerings. Many who came were rich and threw their money in with a flair. Then a poor widow arrived and, a little embarrassed, quickly dropped in two pennies. Jesus called the attention of the disciples to the widow and said, "This poor

119

widow just put in more than all the others. They gave from their abundance, but she gave out of her poverty and put in the last two pennies she had" (Mark 12:41–44).

Outsiders

There were other people in Jerusalem for the Passover besides Jews. Some of these were Greeks who had come to worship. They went over to Philip, who looked like a Galilean. He was standing by the entrance to the Jewish courtyard of the Temple. They said, "Sir, we wish we could see Jesus."

So Philip went and got Andrew, and together they told Jesus. Then Jesus went out into the courtyard of the Gentiles and talked with the men.

When He finished, He went back in and said to His disciples, "The time has come for the Son of Man to die and be glorified. Unless a grain of wheat falls into the ground and dies, it produces nothing; but if it's buried, it will produce many more grains. This is true for everyone. He who loves his life above everything else will lose it, but he who dies to this world will gain life forever. Those who want to be My servants must follow Me, and where I am, that's where they will be. My Father will honor all who are My servants" (John 12:20-26).

God's Voice

Jesus continued, "I am troubled about what lies ahead, but what should I say? 'Father, save Me from this awful hour'? That's the purpose for which I came. Oh, My Father, glorify Your name through Me!"

Then a loud voice from heaven spoke and said, "I have glorified it before, and I will glorify it again." The people heard the voice and some said, "That sounded like thunder." Others said, "No, that sounded like an angel said something to Him."

Jesus said, "That voice was not for My benefit, but for yours. The time has come for the ruler of this world to be judged. When I am lifted up, I will draw all people to Me." By this, Jesus was letting people know that He would be crucified.

Then the people said, "We've been told that according to Scripture, when the Messiah comes, He will stay with us forever. So how can You claim to be the Son of Man if You say they will crucify You?"

Jesus answered, "The light is with you just a few more days. Follow the light, or darkness will overtake you and you won't know which way to go. Believe the light, and you will become sons of light." Then He turned and walked away, and He and His disciples disappeared into the crowd (John 12:27-36).

People Refuse to Believe

Even though Jesus had performed many miracles, most of the people did not believe in Him. Isaiah was right when he asked, "Lord, who has believed our message? To whom has the power of the Lord been revealed but to us?"

The reason so many could not believe was just as Isaiah had said: "God let them close their eyes and harden their hearts. That's why they couldn't see and understand that they should to come to Him to be healed." Isaiah said all this because he foresaw Christ's glory and spoke about Him.

Quite a number of priests and leaders believed in Jesus, but because of the chief priests and the leading Pharisees, they didn't openly confess their faith in Him as the Messiah. This was so that they wouldn't be barred from the synagogue. Besides this, they loved to be praised by their leaders more than to be praised by God.

Then from one end of the Temple Jesus called out, "He who believes in Me not only believes in Me, but also in the One who sent Me. And he who sees Me for who I am also sees the One who sent Me. I have come as light to the world so you won't remain in the dark. If you hear what I'm saying and don't believe Me, I'll not condemn you, because I came to save, not to condemn. He who rejects Me and doesn't believe what I say condemns himself, and my words will stand against Him. I'm not using My own authority when I tell you this; the Father has told Me what to say. And what He is offering you is eternal life. That's why I'm telling you what the Father has told Me" (John 12:37-50).

twenty-two

Jesus Talks About the Future

As Jesus was leaving the Temple, His disciples pointed with pride to its massive stones. He said to them, "The time is coming when not one of the massive stones of the Temple will be left on top of another."

The disciples were stunned by His remark. So when they got to the Mount of Olives, they quietly asked Jesus, "When will this take place? Will there be signs to let us know that the end is coming? Is that when You will set up Your kingdom?"

Jesus answered, "Don't let anyone mislead you. Many will come in My name, claiming to be anointed by God, and will mislead many. Also you will hear of wars breaking out here and there, but don't be alarmed. This has to happen, but it doesn't mean the end. Nations and kingdoms will fight, and there will be famines and earthquakes in different parts of the world. All these things are but birth pains of the world to come.

"You will be persecuted, arrested, thrown into prison, and even killed. You will be hated all over the world because of your loyalty to Me. Many will turn away from Me and will hate and betray one another. Also, false preachers will come and lead many astray. Lawlessness will increase and spread everywhere, and people's love will grow cold. But those who endure to the end will be saved. The good news of the kingdom will be preached all over the world, and then the end will arrive.

"In time you will see happening what Daniel predicted: The power that causes desolation will surround Jerusalem and take its stand in the holy place. Let those who read his prophecy understand and pay attention to what it says. Then those who live in Judea should quickly flee to the mountains. Those outside the house should not take time to go back in and decide what to take. And those in the field should not go back home to get what they need. Those days will be hard on pregnant women and mothers nursing their babies. Pray that you won't have to flee to the mountains during the winter or on the Sabbath.

"In the future there will be days of even greater tribulation. But for the sake of God's people that time will be shortened, or none of them would survive. Be careful! If anyone says to you, 'Look, there is Christ!' or 'Look, He's here!' don't believe it. False christs will come and deceive many, and false prophets will work miracles to trick God's people. I'm telling you this ahead of time so that you won't be misled. So when they tell you that Christ is here or there, don't go looking for Him. As the lightning flashes from east to west and lights up the whole sky, that's how the coming of the Son of Man will be.

"When people see vultures gathering, they know there's a carcass nearby, so also there will be signs that the end is near. In those days the sun will be darkened and the moon will not give its light. The stars will fall and the heavens will be shaken. Then the Son of Man will appear in the clouds of heaven, and people everywhere will weep as they see Him coming in power and great glory. At a blast of the trumpet He will send His angels to gather together His people from one end of the earth to the other.

"Now, learn a lesson from the fig tree. When you see it bud and its leaves begin to appear, you know that spring is here and summer is not far away. So when you see these things begin to happen, you will know that the end is near, standing at the door.

"This generation will not pass from the scene before they see these things happening. And the time is coming when the heavens and the earth you now see will pass away, but what I've said will not.

"No one knows the exact day or hour when the Son of Man will come, not even the angels nor the Son while He is here, but my Father only" (Matt. 24:1-36).

The Last Days

Jesus continued, "Just before the Son of Man returns, it will be as it was in the days of Noah before the Flood. In those days people were living life to the full with eating, drinking, partying, and getting married as often as they wanted, right up to the day that Noah and his family went into the ark. People didn't think what Noah had said would happen, when suddenly the Flood carried them all away. That's how it will be just before the Son of Man comes back.

"In those days, men will be working side by side—one will be ready and the other will not. Women will be busy at home baking and cooking—one will be ready and the other will not. So be prepared, because you don't know when the end will break in on you and the Lord will come.

"If a homeowner knew exactly when a burglar was coming to break into his house, he would watch for him to stop him from breaking in. So stay awake, because if you stop looking for Him, the Son of Man will come when least expected.

"A faithful and sensible servant is one whom his master trusts and gives responsibility to manage his affairs and to look after his family while he's gone. Blessed is that servant when his master returns and finds that he did well. He will put him in charge of everything he owns. But if that servant takes advantage of his master's absence and begins to mistreat the other servants, exploit the family, and eat and drink with his wicked friends, his master will come back unexpectedly and surprise him. He will relieve him of all his responsibilities and put in his record that he's a thief and a liar. That servant's remorse and grief will be beyond words" (Matt. 24:37-51).

Bridesmaids

Jesus continued: "In the end, the kingdom of heaven will be like 10 bridesmaids who took their oil lamps and went outside to wait for the bridegroom. Five were wise and five were foolish. The foolish took no extra oil with them, but the wise did. When the bridegroom's coming was delayed, they all became drowsy and fell asleep.

"At midnight a shout was heard: 'The bridegroom is coming to get his bride! Go out to meet him!'

"They all woke up, lit their lamps, and went out to meet him. Then the foolish ones said to the wise, 'Our lamps are going out! Please give us some of your oil.'

"But the wise said, 'We can't. If we did, there wouldn't be enough for you *and* us. Quick, go to a shop and buy some!'

"While they went looking for oil, the bridegroom came. And those who were ready went with him and his bride to his father's house for the wedding, and the door was shut. A little later, the foolish bridesmaids came, knocked on the door, and said, 'Lord, open the door and let us in!' But he answered, 'I don't recognize your voices. Who are you?'

"So stay awake and always be ready to meet the bridegroom, because you don't know the day or the hour when the door will be shut and the Son of Man will be on His way" (Matt. 25:1-13).

Three Servants

Jesus continued: "At the time of the end, the kingdom of heaven will be like the story of a man going on a business trip. Before he left, he called together three of his most trusted servants and gave each of them some money to invest for him while he was gone. He gave one of them $5,000, the next servant $2,000, and the third servant $1,000, depending on their ability. Then he left.

"The servant who had received $5,000 immediately invested it in the company and soon doubled it. The servant who had received $2,000 did the same thing and soon doubled what he had. But the servant who had received $1,000 did nothing with it. He just kept it in a safe place.

"After some time the man came back to see what his servants had done with his money. The one who had received $5,000 said, 'Sir, I invested what you gave me and doubled it for you.' The master said, 'Well done! You're a good and faithful servant. You invested my money wisely, so I can trust you with much more. When this meeting is over, let's celebrate!'

"Next, the servant who had received $2,000 said, 'Sir, I invested what you gave me and also doubled it for you.' The master replied, 'Well done! You too are a good and faithful servant. You invested my money wisely, so I can trust you with much more. When this meeting is over, let's celebrate!'

"Then the servant who had received $1,000 said, '"Sir, I know you expect a good return on your money. So rather than taking a risk of losing what you gave me, I decided to keep it in a safe place. Here it is.' The master said, 'So you think I require too much? Well, the least you could have done was to put it in the bank to draw interest. I will give it to the one who was responsible for investing the most.

"'To those who know how to invest my money, more will be given. But for those who have done nothing with what I gave them, what they had will be taken away. You have not been a profitable servant. I'll have to let you go.' So they took him out in the dark, where he wept bitterly with deep remorse" (Matt. 25:14-30).

Jesus as Judge

Then Jesus spoke of the final judgment by saying, "When the Son of Man comes in His glory and all the holy angels with Him, He will take His seat as king. All nations will be brought before Him, and He will separate the people as a shepherd does sheep from goats. The sheep will be on his right, and the goats on his left.

"Then the King will say to those on His right, 'Come, you are blessed by My Father. The kingdom is yours. It was set aside for you from the beginning of the world.

"'When I was hungry, you fed Me. When I was thirsty, you gave Me something to drink. When I had no place to lay My head, you invited Me home. When I needed clothes, you gave them to Me. When I was sick, you cared for Me. And when I was in prison, you visited Me.'

"The righteous will say, 'Lord, when did we see You hungry, thirsty, without a place to stay, and needing clothes? When did we find You sick or in prison and do all this for You?'

"The King will answer, 'When you did it for others, especially for those who love Me, it was as if you had done it for Me.'

"Then the King will say to those on His left, 'Leave My presence! You don't really belong to Me. You, together with the devil and his angels, will have to be destroyed in the lake of fire. When I was hungry, you didn't feed Me. When I was thirsty, you didn't give Me something to drink. When I had no place to lay My head, you didn't invite Me home. When I needed clothes, you didn't give Me any. When I was sick, you didn't care. And when I was in prison, you didn't visit Me.'

"They will protest, 'Lord, we didn't know You were hungry, thirsty, needing a place to stay and clothes, sick or in prison. If we had, we would have helped You.'

"The King will say, 'When you didn't help others, especially those who love Me, you didn't help Me.' Then they will be taken away to be destroyed forever, but the righteous will be given eternal life" (Matt. 25:31–46).

twenty three

The Last Days of Jesus

It was now time for the Passover, followed by the weeklong Festival of Unleavened Bread. So Jesus told Peter and John to prepare for the Passover meal so they could all eat together. They asked, "Lord, where do You want to have the meal?"

Jesus answered, "Go down to the city, and as you go through the gates, you will see a man carrying a large clay jar of water on his head. Follow him to where he's going. Then knock on the door of that house and say to the owner, 'Sir, the Teacher was wondering if He could use your guestroom so He and His disciples can eat the Passover meal together.' The man will take you upstairs to a large room already set up for that purpose. That's the place. Then go and get things ready for us."

They went into the city, and everything happened just as Jesus had said. So they got things ready.

The Passover Meal

When all the disciples got there, Jesus said to them, "I've been looking forward to eating this Passover meal with you because it will be our last time together before I die. I will not eat it with you again until everything is accomplished and we're in the kingdom of God" (Luke 22:7-16).

Jesus knew that the time had come for Him to leave this world and go back home to the Father. Having loved His own people all the years He was here, He loved them to the very end.

It was now time to eat together, but the devil had entered the heart of Judas Iscariot to betray Jesus. Jesus understood His own mission, and He knew that He had come from God, that the Father had given Him authority to do what He did, and that He would go back to God. So He got up from the table, removed His outer robe, poured water into a basin, and began to wash the disciples' feet, then dried them with a towel He had wrapped around His waist.

When He came to Peter, Peter objected. "Lord, You're going to wash my feet? You are the Son of God!"

Jesus replied, "You don't understand why I'm doing this, but you will."

Peter protested, "I will not let You stoop to wash my feet!"

Jesus responded, "If you don't let Me wash your feet, you cannot belong to Me."

Peter said, "Lord, if that's the case, then wash not only my feet but my hands and my head!"

Jesus assured him, "When a person has taken a bath and then walked down the road and back, all he needs to do is to wash the dust off his feet to be completely clean. All of you are clean, except one." He said this because He knew that Judas had already planned to betray Him.

After washing the disciples' feet, Jesus put His outer robe back on, sat down, and said, "Do you know why I washed your feet? You call Me 'Lord,' and you're right, because I am. If I'm willing to wash your feet, you ought to be willing to wash one another's feet. I've given you an example. You should do for each other what I have done for you. A servant is not greater than his master, neither is a messenger greater than the one who sent him. If you understand these things and do them, you are blessed indeed.

"What I'm going to say next doesn't apply to all of you. I chose each of you, except one, because I knew your hearts. But the scripture that says 'The one who eats with Me has turned against Me' must be fulfilled. I'm telling you this before it happens so when it does, it will strengthen your faith in who I am. Whoever accepts from you the truth about Me accepts Me, and whoever accepts Me accepts the Father who sent Me" (John 13:1-20).

Taking one of the flat loaves of bread, Jesus asked God's blessing on it. Then He broke it into 12 pieces, giving each disciple a piece, and said, "Take it and eat. It's a symbol of My body." Next He took the cup in front of Him, gave thanks to God, and turning to the disciples, said, "Each of you drink from it. It is a symbol of My blood, which fulfills God's covenant and the forgiveness of sin. I will not drink of the fruit of the vine again until I drink it with you in My Father's kingdom" (Matt. 26:26-29).

After Jesus said this, He became deeply distressed and said, "The truth is that one of you will betray Me!"

The disciples looked at each other in shock, wondering which one it could be. John, the beloved disciple, was sitting next to Jesus, and Peter motioned to him to ask Jesus who it was. John leaned over and quietly asked Jesus, "Lord, who is it?"

Jesus whispered, "The one to whom I will give this piece of bread after I dip it in the sauce." After He did, He offered it to Judas, who took it. As soon as he did, Satan entered into Judas's heart and took full control. Jesus said to him, "What you're going to do, do quickly."

None of the disciples knew what Jesus meant when He said that. Some thought that because Judas was in charge of the money, Jesus was telling him to hurry off and buy whatever else was needed for the Passover, or to go and give an offering for the poor. Judas quickly left and went out into the dark (John 13:21-30).

The Evening's Conversation

After Judas had left, Jesus said, "The time has come for the Son of Man to bring glory to God by letting Him glorify Me through all that will happen. I will be with you only a little while longer. I'm telling you what I have told the Jewish leaders: 'Where I'm going you cannot come.'

"I'm giving you a new commandment: Love each other as much as I have loved you. That's how you should love each other. And that's how people will know that you are My disciples."

Peter said, "Lord, where are You going?"

Jesus answered, "You can't come with Me now, but you will follow Me later."

Peter responded, "Lord, why can't I follow You now? I'm willing to die for You!"

Jesus replied, "You say you're willing to die for Me? Let Me tell you that before the rooster crows twice in the morning, you will have denied knowing Me three times."

Then He continued: "But don't let your hearts be troubled by what you will see. You believe in God, so don't lose your faith in Me. My Father's house can't be destroyed. And there's plenty of room for everyone. If it were not so, I would have told you. I'll be going to prepare a place for you, and if I do that, you can be sure that I'll come back to take you home with Me so that we can be together. You know where I'm going, and you know how to get there."

Thomas spoke up and said, "Lord, we don't know where You're going, so how can we know how to get there?"

Jesus answered, "I'm the way. And I'm the truth and the life. No one can find their way to the Father except through Me. If from the first you had known Me as you should have, you would have known the Father also. But now you have seen Him."

Then Philip said, "Lord, give us a glimpse of the Father and we'll be content."

Jesus replied, "Philip, don't you even yet know Me well enough to see the Father? Why are you asking to see Him? Don't you believe that the Father is in Me and I in Him? What I've been saying came not from Me but from the Father. And the things I've done I didn't do on My own—the Father who is in Me did them. Believe Me when I tell you that the Father is in Me and that I am in the Father. If you have a hard time believing this, then at least believe in Me because of what you've seen Me do.

"He who believes in Me will do the works that I have done, but even more extensively, because I'm leaving and going to the Father. And whatever you ask for in My name, I will do it to honor the Father, so that the Father, not I, will receive the glory" (Mark 14:27-31; John 13:31-14:14).

Conversations About the Holy Spirit

Jesus continued: "If you love Me, you will obey Me and keep My commandments. And I will ask the Father to send you another helper, the Holy Spirit, who will never leave you. He will lead you into more truth. The world doesn't listen to the Holy Spirit; that's why the world can't know Him. But you know Him because He's in your heart, and He will live in you.

"I'm not going to leave you alone. I will come and help you. For a little while the world will not see Me, but I will live again, and then *you'll* feel like living again. I'll be going to the Father, and in your hearts you'll be there too, because I'm in you and you're in Me.

"Those who obey Me and keep My commandments are the ones who love Me and are loved by My Father. And I will reveal more and more of Myself to them."

Then Thaddaeus (sometimes called Judas) spoke up: "Lord, how can You reveal Yourself to us and the world not see You?"

Jesus answered, "All those who love Me and keep My command-ments, My Father and I will love and will make Our home in their hearts. Those who don't love Me will not listen to Me. These words are not My own; it's the Father who is speaking through Me. I'm telling you these things while I'm still here.

"The Father will send the Holy Spirit to help you. He will take My place and teach you more things and will remind you of what I've said to you.

"Peace I leave with you, but not the kind the world gives. My peace is deeper. So don't be afraid or let your hearts be troubled. I have to go away, but I'll come back. If you really love Me, you'll be happy for Me, because I'm going home to the Father, who is greater than I am. I have told you these things before they happen so that when they do, your faith in Me will be even stronger than it was before.

"We don't have much more time to talk, because the devil, who thinks he rules the world, has found nothing in Me that responds to him. I love the Father and do only what He tells Me to do. The world needs to know this. So come, let's go" (John 14:15-31).

twenty-four

A Long Night

After the Passover meal, Jesus and His disciples sang a hymn and left the city for the Mount of Olives. As they were walking along, Jesus said to them, "Tonight when they come to arrest Me, all of you will run. As the scripture says: 'They will smite the Shepherd, and the sheep will scatter.' But I will always love you. After I rise from the grave, I will go up to Galilee and meet you there."

Peter said, "Even though they all run, I will not!"

Jesus replied, "Let Me remind you what I told you earlier—that before the rooster crows twice you will deny Me three times."

Peter spoke up even more strongly: "If I have to die with You, I will not run!" Then all of them said the same thing (Mark 14:26-31).

Jesus said, "Simon, Simon! Satan wants to shake your faith in Me, like chaff is sifted from wheat. But I have prayed for you that your faith in Me will not totally fail. You will recover, and when you do, strengthen the faith of your brothers" (Luke 22:31, 32).

As they continued on their way, Jesus pointed to a grapevine and said, "I am the enduring vine, and my Father is the vineyard owner. He cuts off every branch that does not bear fruit, and prunes those that do so that they will produce more fruit. You've already been pruned once just by My being here and teaching you. Stay connected to Me, and I will stay connected to you. You can't produce fruit by yourself.

"I am God's vine, and you are the branches. Those attached to Me will produce much fruit. Without Me you can't produce a thing. Those not attached to Me are like useless branches that are cut off and thrown away. People put them in piles and burn them up. But if you stay attached to Me and keep what I've said in your heart, whatever you ask for to produce more fruit, it will be given to you, and my Father will be glorified. This is what makes you My disciples. So love one another" (John 15:1-17).

Rejection

"If the people of this world hate you, remember that they hated Me before they hated you. If you had the same spirit as the world, people would love you, but you don't. Remember what I have told you: 'A servant is not greater than his master.' They rejected Me, so they'll reject you. But some accepted Me and believed what I said, so some will accept you and believe what you say.

"Those who mistreat you won't do it so much because they hate you, but because you belong to Me. They don't know that the Father sent Me. If I had not come and pointed out their sins, they would not be guilty. But now they have no excuse for not knowing what sin is. That's why they don't like Me or My Father. If I had neither worked miracles nor done anything different from their teachers, they would not be guilty of rejecting Me. But they saw everything I did and still hated Me and My Father for what We did. As the scripture says: 'They hated Me without cause.'

"I will send the Holy Spirit to come to help you. With the Father's consent, He will take charge, and what He says about Me is true. He will help you to tell others about Me and what you have seen Me do, because you have been with Me from the beginning of My ministry.

"I'm telling you this so that you won't be surprised at what will happen to you. They will expel you from the synagogue and will not hesitate to kill you, thinking that they're doing a service to God. They will do this because they don't really know the Father or Me. When that time comes, remember what I told you. I didn't tell you this earlier, because I knew I would be with you a while longer" (John 15:18-16:4).

The Holy Spirit

Jesus continued: "I'm going away, yet none of you insists on knowing where I'm going. I'm going back to the Father who sent Me. But you're not happy for Me—you're sad. Actually, it's best for you that I go away, because if I don't, the Holy Spirit can't take over. But when I go back to the Father, I will send Him to you.

"And when He comes, He will go ahead of you, convicting people of their sins, urging them to turn to God and live a righteous life, and warning them of judgment to come because they didn't accept Me. The Holy Spirit will do all this because I go to the Father. Remember that Satan has already been judged.

"I could tell you a lot more, but that's enough for now. When the Holy Spirit comes, He will guide you into all truth. He will not take the initiative, use his own authority, or do things according to His own ideas, but will say only what He has been told, which includes telling you of things to come. He will talk, not about Himself, but about Me and whatever I tell Him to say. I have done what the Father has asked Me to do. That's why I said that I will send the Holy Spirit and that He will continue my mission and do what I ask Him to do" (John 16:5-15).

Sorrow and Joy

Then Jesus said, "My time is almost up. Soon I'll have to leave you, and you won't see Me. Then you'll see Me again for a little while before I go to the Father."

The disciples asked each other, "What does He mean when He says, 'You won't see Me and then you'll see Me for a little while before I go to the Father'? We don't understand."

Jesus overheard their discussion and asked, "Are you wondering what I meant when I said, 'You won't see Me, and then you'll see Me'? You will be deeply hurt and will weep when you see what they are going to do to Me. Others will rejoice. But your sorrow will soon turn to joy.

"It's like when a woman is about to have a baby. It begins with labor pains. She knows she has to go through it. But as soon as the baby comes, she forgets all her pain for the joy she has because of the new life she has brought into the world.

"So you'll be hurting when you see what happens to Me, but I will see you again, and you will rejoice. No one will be able to take that joy away from you. Then you'll have no more questions about these things. And if you need anything to carry out your mission, you can go directly to the Father and ask Him for it in My name and He'll give it to you. You haven't done this before. Ask and you will receive. Then you'll have even more joy" (John 16:16-24).

The Father

Jesus continued: "I've talked to you about these things before, using parables and figures of speech, but soon I'll talk to you plainly about the Father. Then you'll know that you can go to the Father directly and ask for things in My name. I won't have to ask Him for you. The Father loves you very much because you love Me and believe that I came from God. I came here from the Father, and when I leave, I'll go back to Him."

The disciples said, "Now You're making things plain, and we're beginning to understand. You know things about the future that others don't know. That's why we don't have to ask someone else. This is what convinces us that You came from God."

Jesus responded, "Are you sure you believe in Me? In a few hours you'll all scatter and leave Me alone. Yet I am not alone, because the

Father is with Me. I've shared these things with you so that you can have the same peace that I have. In the world you'll have many troubles and trials, but take heart, because I have overcome the world, and so will you" (John 16:25-33).

Then Jesus looked up to heaven and prayed, "Father, the time has come. Honor Me as Your Son so that I can bring honor to You and glorify Your name. You have given Me authority over everything, including the right to give eternal life to all who accept Me. This is eternal life—to know You, the only true God, and Jesus Christ, whom You have sent.

"I have honored You and brought glory to Your name by doing everything You've asked Me to do. I'm about to finish My work. Then We'll be together again, and I'll share the same glory with You that I had before the world began.

"I've lived out Your life for all to see and have told these men all about You. They were part of this world, but You gave them to Me to be My disciples, and they have obeyed Your word. Everything I have You have given to Me, and what You have told Me I have passed on to them. They've accepted what I told them about You, because they believe that I came from You and that You sent Me. I pray for everyone in the world, but especially for these men, because they belong to You and You have given them to Me. So they are Mine and will bring glory to My name.

"Father, soon I'll be leaving this world and coming back home to You. But these men will be here alone. Please watch over them and help them to be one, as We are one. While I've been here, I've kept them together so that not one of them would be lost, except Judas, just as the Scriptures foretold.

"I'm ready to finish My work and come home. I've told these men what You wanted Me to so that they would have the same joy of knowing You as I have. But the world hates them because they're not part of the world, just as I'm not. Father, I'm not asking You to take them out of this world, but to keep them from being overcome by the evil one. They don't belong here, just as I don't. Set these men apart from the world through the truth, which is Your word. I'm sending them into the world for the same reason You have sent Me. I have set Myself apart for them so they may set themselves apart for You.

"I pray not only for these men, but for all those who will believe in Me because of what these men will tell them about Me. I pray that all of them will be united and be one with Us, just as You and I are one, so that the world will see it and believe that You sent Me. I have shared with these men the glory You have given Me so that they can be perfectly united, as We are. That is how the world will know that You sent Me and that You love them as You love Me.

"Father, I want these men to be with Me in heaven to see the glory that I had with You from the beginning and how much You love Me. Righteous Father, the world doesn't know You as I do, but these men know that You sent me. I've shown them what You are like, and have told them about You. I will continue to tell them about You so that the same love You have for Me will be in them, just as I am in them" (John 17:1-26).

Gethsemane

As they were making their way to the olive grove called Gethsemane, on the western slope of the Mount of Olives, Jesus said to His disciples, "Stay here and pray for Me while I go to pray. I won't be very far away." He felt so depressed that He decided to take Peter, James, and John with Him for encouragement. They walked a little ways before He said to them, "I feel as if the life is being crushed right out of Me. Stay here and really pray earnestly for Me."

He went a little farther, fell on His face, and in agony of spirit prayed, "O My Father, please don't let Me drink this cup of suffering! Yet I want to do not My will, but Yours."

Then He went back to the three disciples and found them sleeping. He quietly nudged Peter awake and said, "Can't you stay awake and pray for Me even for an hour? You need to pray for Me and for yourself so that the devil won't overpower you. I know the heart is willing, but the body calls for sleep."

He went back a second time and prayed even more intently, "O My Father, if You want Me to drink this cup of suffering, Your will be done." Then He returned to the three disciples and again found them sleeping. They just could not stay awake. So He let them sleep and went away to pray a third time (Matt. 26:36-44).

Again Jesus fell on His face and cried out to God. He was in such agony that great drops of sweat tinged with blood broke out and ran down His face to the ground. He was at the point of dying when an angel from heaven came and gave Him the strength He needed to carry out His Father's will (Luke 22:43, 44).

He got to His feet and went back to the three disciples, woke them up, and said, "You're still sleeping? You need to get up. It's time for the Son of Man to be betrayed and turned over to sinful men. My betrayer is looking for Me—let's go to meet him." Together they went to the other disciples and awakened them too.

Meanwhile, Judas had already found the olive grove and, together with the leading priests and elders, was looking for Jesus. They were followed by Temple guards and soldiers armed with swords, and a wild mob carrying clubs. Judas had said to the priests, "The one I kiss is the one you want. Grab Him!"

Jesus knew that they were coming for Him, so He went to meet them. When Judas saw Him, he said, "Hello, Master!" and went up and kissed Him.

Jesus looked at him and said, "Friend, why have you come to see Me?" Then the Temple guards stepped forward and grabbed Jesus (Matt. 26:45-50; Luke 22:52).

When Peter saw this, he pulled out his short sword and swung it at the nearest man. The man ducked, but Peter sliced off his right ear. The man's name was Malchus, one of the servants of the high priest. Jesus turned to Peter and said, "Put away your sword, Peter. If you fight by the sword, you'll be killed by the sword. Don't you know that I could ask the Father for help and He would send thousands of angels to protect Me? But then how would the Scriptures be fulfilled?"

Jesus then reached out and touched Malchus' head, and restored his ear (Matt. 26:51-54; John 18:10; Luke 22:51).

Then Jesus asked the guards, "For whom are you looking?"

They barked, "Jesus of Nazareth!"

He answered, "I am Jesus." When He said that, they all fell to the ground. When they got up, He asked the same question.

They answered, "We want Jesus of Nazareth!"

He said, "I told you that I am Jesus. Arrest Me and let these men go" (John 18:6-8).

When the disciples heard that, they all turned and ran. A young follower of Jesus decided to stay by, and one of the soldiers reached out to grab him, but he twisted out of the linen tunic, left it behind, and ran away naked (Mark 14:50, 51).

Arrest at Midnight

Then the captain of the guard ordered his men to arrest Jesus. They grabbed Him, tied His hands behind His back, and led Him away. They first took Him for a preliminary trial to the palace of Annas, the retired high priest. He was the father-in-law of Caiaphas, the official high priest, who earlier had said, "It's better for one man to die than for a whole nation to perish."

Peter and another disciple had sneaked back and followed the soldiers at a distance. When they got to the palace gate, the woman at the gate recognized the other disciple and let him in, but not Peter. After the disciple turned and saw Peter still outside, he went and talked to the woman, and she let Peter in. As she did, she asked, "You're one of Jesus' disciples, aren't you?" Peter stated strongly, "I am not!" And a rooster crowed. Then he went over to the fire, where some of the officers and servants of the high priest were warming themselves.

Inside, Annas asked Jesus about His disciples and what He had been teaching. Jesus answered, "What I teach is widely known. I've taught in the synagogues, in the Temple where the Jewish leaders were, and out in public. I've never taught anything in secret that I've not taught openly for all to hear. They can tell you what I said."

When Jesus said that, one of the officers struck him in the face and said, "Is that the way You talk to the high priest?"

Jesus answered, "If I said something wrong or spoke disrespectfully, tell Me. Don't just slap Me for nothing."

Then Annas told the guards to take Jesus through the courtyard to Caiaphas, who was meeting with the Jewish high council called the Sanhedrin.

Outside in the courtyard, Peter was standing by the fire warming himself. Someone looked at him and asked, "Aren't you one of Jesus' disciples?"

Again Peter declared, "No, I'm not."

Then one of the servants of the high priest, a relative of Malchus, whose ear Peter had cut off, said, "Didn't I see you in the olive grove with Jesus? You sound like one of those Galileans!"

Peter cursed and said vehemently, "I told you I don't know the man!" Just then the rooster crowed a second time (John 18:18-27; Matt. 26:57-59; Mark 14:70, 71).

Then Peter remembered what Jesus had said: "Before the rooster crows twice, you will deny knowing me three times." When Peter realized what he had done, he was so heartbroken that he rushed out the gate, weeping bitterly (Matt. 26:75; Mark 14:72).

The Night Trial

Caiaphas had called an emergency meeting of the members of the Jewish high council, those whom he had selectively contacted. So the chief priest and council members decided to find witnesses who were willing to lie about Jesus so that they could convict Him before daybreak, and before people could find out what was happening. Even though many came forward with false testimonies, the members couldn't agree enough whether to give Jesus the death penalty or not. Finally two men said, "We heard this fellow say, 'I am able to destroy God's Temple, and in three days I'll be able to rebuild it.'"

When the high priest heard this, he stood up and said to Jesus,

"Aren't You going to defend Yourself? Didn't You hear what these men said about You?"

Jesus just stood there quietly and made no response.

Then the high priest said, "I'm putting You under oath. Tell us, are You the Messiah, the Son of God?"

Jesus answered, "You said it. Yes, I am. One day you will see the Son of Man sitting on the right hand of God, coming back with full power and authority."

Upon hearing this, Caiaphas took the edge of his outer robe, ripped it open, and shouted, "We don't need more evidence! You've heard what He said. What's your verdict?" They all shouted, "Guilty! He deserves to die!" (Matt. 26:59-66).

Then the mob in the courtroom pushed forward and spit in Jesus' face. They blindfolded Him, hit Him with their fists, beat Him with sticks, and shouted in His ears, "If You're the Messiah, prophesy! Tell us, who hit You?"

When Jesus did not answer, they cursed Him and spoke many other things against Him (Luke 22:63-65).

twenty-five

Daybreak

At the first light of dawn, when all the members of the high council were there for the official trial, they ordered Jesus brought back into the courtroom. They demanded, "Are You the Messiah? Tell us!"

Jesus answered, "If I tell you, you won't believe Me. Even if I offered to discuss the question with you, you wouldn't answer Me. But the time is coming when you will see the Son of Man sitting at the right hand of God, having great power and authority."

Then they all asked at once, "Are you saying that You're the Son of God?"

Jesus replied, "You said it correctly. I am."

When they heard that, they began shouting, "We don't need another witness. We heard what He said. He's condemned Himself!" (Luke 22:66-71).

When Judas, who was in the crowded courtroom, realized that Jesus was about to receive the death sentence, he was overwhelmed with anguish and guilt for what he had done. He pressed through the crowd to the high priest, held out the 30 pieces of silver, and cried, "I have sinned! I have betrayed an innocent man!"

The council members said coolly, "That's your problem, not ours." Judas then threw the 30 pieces of silver on the floor and went out and hanged himself.

The leading priests picked up the money but were puzzled over what to do with it. They said to each other, "We can't put this money into the Temple treasury. It's against the law to use blood money." So they decided to buy an old pottery field and turn it into a cemetery for foreigners. That's why it's called the Cemetery of Blood.

This was according to Jeremiah's prophecy, which said, "They took 30 pieces of silver, the value they placed on him, and bought an old pottery field" (Matt. 27:3-10).

Before Pilate

It was still early morning when Caiaphas and the council members took Jesus to the Roman governor's residence to get Pilate's approval of the recommended death penalty. But they wouldn't go into the judgment hall, because that would make them ritually unclean and prevent them from taking part in the Passover.

So Pilate came out on the balcony overlooking the courtyard and asked, "Why are you bringing this Man to me so early? What are you accusing Him of? And what's so urgent that you have to bring Him to me before my day even begins?"

They replied, "If He were not a dangerous criminal, we wouldn't have brought Him so early."

Pilate responded, "Judge Him according to your own law."

They said, "But it's against the law for us to put someone to death without the approval of Rome" (John 18:28-32).

Then they stated their case and accused Jesus of ruining the country by telling people that He was the Messiah and not to pay taxes to Caesar. When Pilate heard this, he had Jesus brought into the judgment hall and asked Him, "Are You the rightful king of the Jews?"

Jesus answered, "You stated it correctly" (Luke 23:2, 3).

Then Jesus asked Pilate, "Are you questioning Me because you want to know more about Me, or because others have raised the question?"

Pilate replied, "Am I a Jew? Why should I be interested in Your kingship? Your own people have rejected You. So what have You done?"

Jesus answered, "My kingdom is not of this world. If it were, My servants would have fought to keep Me from being arrested and turned over to the Jews. But My kingdom is not here."

Pilate responded, "So You are a king?"

Jesus answered, "You're right. I am. For that reason I was born and came into this world to tell people the truth about God. Those who love the truth listen and can tell it's the truth."

Pilate stood to his feet and said, "Truth? What is truth?" Then he went back outside and said to the Jewish religious leaders, "I find nothing about this Man that would call for the death penalty" (John 18:34-38).

When Pilate heard the priests say something about Galilee, he asked if Jesus was a Galilean, and they told him He was. So he sent Jesus to Herod, who was in charge of Galilee and visiting Jerusalem at the time because of the Passover (Luke 23:6, 7).

Before Herod

Herod was glad to see Jesus. He had wanted to meet Him for some time because he had heard so many things about Jesus and was hoping to see Him perform a miracle. Although Herod questioned Him extensively, Jesus refused to answer. The chief priests and the mob had followed Jesus through the streets to Herod's palace. When Jesus refused to answer, they became angry and began shouting all kinds of accusations against Him. Then Herod's guards started making fun of Jesus, and soon Herod himself joined in. This went on for some time. Finally Herod ordered the guards to put one of his royal robes on Jesus, and sent Him back to Pilate.

From that day on, Pilate and Herod became the best of friends, whereas before they had been bitter enemies (Luke 23:8-12).

Before Pilate Again

At the Passover it was the custom of the Roman governor to release to the Jews one prisoner of their choice. One of the prisoners was a man named Barabbas, who was convicted of starting a rebellion against Rome and using his followers to commit murder. After Jesus has been brought back from Herod and the priests, and the mob had quieted down, Pilate said, "I'll give you a choice. Whom do you want me to release to you, Barabbas or Jesus?" (Matt. 27:15-17; Mark 15:7).

They shouted, "Barabbas!"

Pilate, determined to release Jesus, ordered Him scourged, hoping to satisfy the Jews. So the soldiers took Jesus to their barracks courtyard and decided to have some quick fun. They made a crown of thorns, forced it on His head, carefully arranged the purple robe on His shoulders, put a rod in His hand as a scepter, and knelt down in front of Him, yelling, "Hail, King of the Jews!" They got up, spit in His face, struck Him with their fists, and took the stick out of His hand and beat Him over the head. Then they took the robe off, scourged Him, and took Him back to Pilate.

Pilate went outside again and said to the Jews, "Take a look at this Man! Does that satisfy you? I want you to know that I find no fault in Him."

When the chief priests and Temple officers saw Jesus, they shouted, "Crucify Him! Crucify Him!"

Pilate responded, "*You* take the responsibility and crucify Him. I told you—I find no fault in Him" (John 18:40-19:6; Matt. 27:27-30).

Pilate knew that they were envious of Jesus, and because of a religious controversy they wanted Him put to death. While he was carrying out his duties as judge, Pilate's wife sent him a note saying, "Have nothing to do with convicting this Man! I've been troubled all day because of a dream about Him last night."

By this time the chief priests and elders had persuaded the crowd to shout as loudly as they could for the release of Barabbas. So when Pilate asked, "Which of these two men standing before you should I let go?" they shouted, "Barabbas!"

Pilate asked, "What should I do with Jesus?"

The crowd shouted back, "Crucify Him!"

Pilate responded, "Why? He hasn't committed any crime worthy of death."

They shouted even louder, "Crucify Him!" (Matt. 27:18–23).

Then the Jewish leaders said, "According to our law, He must be put to death because He claims to be the Son of God." When Pilate heard this, he was afraid who Jesus might really be. So he took Him inside and asked, "Where did You come from?"

Jesus didn't answer.

Pilate asked again, "Aren't You going to say something? Don't You know I have the power to crucify You and the power to let You go?"

Jesus answered, "The power you have was given to you. On your own you couldn't do anything. But those who delivered Me to you have the greater sin."

Pilate went back out and again tried to release Him. But the Jewish leaders reminded him that if he released a man who claimed to be king, he would no longer be a friend of Caesar's. When Pilate heard this, he took his seat as judge and proceeded with the trial.

It was Friday morning, the preparation day for the weekly Sabbath. Pilate told the guards to bring Jesus out.

He looked at the crowd and said, "Here is your King! Take a good look at Him!"

When the people saw Jesus, they shouted, "Crucify Him!"

Pilate responded, "Do you want me to crucify your King?"

The Jewish leaders cried out, "We have no king but Caesar" (John 19:7–15).

Crucifixion

Pilate was forced to make a decision, so he turned Jesus over to the Roman troops for crucifixion. The soldiers took Jesus away, scourged Him again, then laid the heavy wooden cross on His shoulders and led Him through the streets of Jerusalem toward Golgatha, the "place of the skull," to be crucified. Two criminals were to be crucified with Him—one on the right and one on the left, with Jesus in the center (John 19:16–18).

After the two scourgings and the heavy blood loss, Jesus was too weak to carry the cross all the way. So the soldiers pulled a man named Simon from the crowd and put the beam on him. He was from the country of Cyrene and was visiting Jerusalem at the time.

A great crowd followed Jesus, including many women who wept at what they were seeing. He turned to them and said, "Daughters of Jerusalem, don't cry for Me; weep for your children and your people. The days are coming when you will say, 'How fortunate are the women who have no children to raise or breast-feed!' Others will look at the surrounding hills and mountains and wish they would fall on them to bury them. If a green tree like Me is being treated this way, what will the Roman soldiers do to the dead trees in Israel?" (Luke 23:26-31).

When they came to Calvary, they offered Jesus some drugged wine to kill the pain, but He refused to drink it. So they went ahead with the crucifixion. As they were nailing Jesus to the cross, He said, "Father, forgive these men. They don't know what they're doing."

Then they hoisted the crosses in place. This was about nine o'clock Friday morning (Mark 15:23-25; Luke 23:32, 33).

Now Pilate had ordered a sign nailed to the top of Jesus' cross that read, "Jesus of Nazareth, King of the Jews." It was written in Greek, Latin, and Aramaic for all to read. When the leading Jews, who were watching from a distance, saw this, they immediately went to Pilate and said, "The sign should read 'He said, I'm the King of the Jews.'"

Pilate answered, "What I have written stands written."

After the soldiers had hoisted the crosses in place, they took Jesus' clothes and divided them into four parts, one for each soldier who had crucified Him. But when they looked at His seamless outer robe, they decided not to cut it up but to gamble for it. This is what the Scripture had said would happen: "They divided my garments among them and gambled for my robe" (John 19:19-24).

As happened during such executions, people from everywhere came to curse the criminals. So they cursed Jesus and said, "You're the one who said You could destroy the Temple and rebuild it in three days. Why don't You save Yourself? If You're the Son of God, come down from the cross."

Also, the chief priests and elders standing at a distance made fun of Him, saying, "If He's the King of Israel, let Him come down from the cross—then we'll believe Him. He put His trust in God. Let God come and deliver Him, for He said He was the Son of God."

The two criminals who were crucified with Jesus said some of the same things. One of them began cursing Him, saying, "If You're the Messiah, save Yourself and us!"

But the other one said, "Don't you have any fear of God? In a few hours we'll be dead and will have to face the judgment. We'll be getting what we deserve. But this Man, Jesus, is not a criminal."

He then turned to Jesus and said, "Lord, don't forget me when You set up Your kingdom."

Jesus answered, "I give you My word this day, you will be with Me in My kingdom (Matt. 27:39-44; Luke 23:39-43).

Standing near the cross was Jesus' mother; her sister; Mary, the wife of Clopas; and Mary Magdalene. When Jesus saw His mother crying, He said, "Mother, don't cry. John is standing next to you. He'll take care of you. Let him be your son in My place."

Then Jesus said to John, "Make My mother your mother, and take care of her for Me," which John did from that day on (John 19:25-27).

About noon, dark clouds suddenly rolled in, covering all of Jerusalem and the surrounding area. It was so dark that the sun seemed to be blotted out. This darkness continued until three o'clock in the afternoon. That's when Jesus cried out, "Eli, Eli, lama sabachthani?" that is, "My God, My God, why have You forsaken Me?"

Some said, "It sounds as if He's calling for Elijah to help Him." Someone standing nearby ran over to the bucket of cheap wine, dipped in a sponge, and put it on a stick to offer Jesus a drink. The others said, "Leave Him alone. Let's see if Elijah will come and help him" (Matt. 27:45-49).

Jesus knew He was about to die. Weakly He said, "I am thirsty." One of the soldiers put the wine-filled sponge on a stick and pushed it against Jesus' mouth. (John 19:28, 29).

After that, Jesus cried out with a loud voice, "Father, into Your hands I commit My spirit! It is finished!" Then He bowed His head and died (Luke 23:46; John 19:30).

And the heavy curtain separating the holy place from the Most Holy Place in the Temple ripped in two from top to bottom. There was a tremendous earthquake, the ground cracked, and huge rocks broke off the mountains. Even some of the graves in the cemetery split open.

The soldiers were terrified. Even their captain said fearfully, "There's no doubt that this Man was the Son of God!" (Matt. 27:51-54).

twenty-six

The Long Weekend

The Jewish leaders didn't want Jesus and the two criminals to be hanging on the cross during the Sabbath, which was also the Passover. So they went to Pilate, asking him to order the soldiers to break the legs of those who had been crucified, so that they would die quickly. He agreed, so the soldiers broke the legs of the two criminals first. But when they came to Jesus, He was already dead. To make sure, a soldier took his spear and pierced Jesus' side, and immediately blood and water flowed out, showing that He was dead.

I, John, was there and saw it. I'm telling you the truth, so that you can know and believe that Jesus really did die. All this happened just as the Scriptures said: "Not one of his bones will be broken" and "They will look at him whose side was pierced" (John 19:31-37).

Friday Afternoon

All this took place on Friday, and the Sabbath would begin in a few hours. A prominent and wealthy council member named Joseph of Arimathea had, with others, been looking forward to the coming kingdom of God. Courageously he went to Pilate and asked for the body of Jesus. Pilate was surprised that Jesus was already dead. To make sure, he called for the officer in charge of the crucifixion and asked him how long Jesus had been dead. When he was satisfied that Jesus had not just passed out, he gave Joseph permission to take the body and bury it (Mark 15:42-45).

Joseph thanked Pilate, and when he got back to Calvary, Nicodemus was there with about 100 pounds of burial supplies, including sheets, spices, and various kinds of ointments. They took Jesus' body down from the cross, wrapped it in spices and linen cloths, and prepared it for burial according to Jewish custom. Not far away was a small garden with a new tomb that belonged to Joseph. That's where they buried Jesus. This was all done on the preparation day, before the Sabbath began (John 19:38-42).

Some of the women followers of Jesus from Galilee, Mary his mother, and Mary Magdelene, stayed by to watch them take the body of Jesus to the tomb and lay it out. Then they went home and prepared spices and fragrant oils to take to the tomb first thing Sunday morning. And when the Sabbath began, they rested according to the commandment (Luke 23:55, 56).

Sabbath

Even though it was Sabbath, the Jewish leaders called a meeting and decided to see Pilate. They said, "Sir, we remember that when Jesus was still alive, He told His disciples, 'After three days I will rise from the dead.' So could you put a Roman seal on the tomb and station a guard there until the third day? We're concerned that His disciples might steal His body and tell the people that He rose from the dead. If that happens, things will be worse than they were before."

Pilate answered, "You may have your guard. Take them and see to it that the tomb is secure. They'll guard it for you. Now be on your way." So they went and watched as the soldiers secured the stone and put a Roman seal on the ropes that held it in place. Then the soldiers stayed there to guard it (Matt. 27:62-66).

After the sun had set, Mary Magdalene; Mary, the mother of another James; and Salome, the wife of Zebedee, went and bought more spices and oils to take to the tomb first thing in the morning (Mark 16:1).

Sunday Morning

As soon as the sun came up early on Sunday, the first day of the week, the women decided to go to the tomb. As they walked, they said to each other, "Who is going to roll away the huge stone for us when we get there?" (Mark 16:2, 3).

While they were on their way, another earthquake struck the area as the angel of the Lord came down from heaven, rolled away the stone, and sat on it. His face was as bright as lightning and his robe as white as snow. When the guards saw him, they shook with fear, then fell to the ground as if they were dead (Matt. 28:1-4).

Now Mary Magdalene had left home earlier, while it was still dark, and got to the tomb first. When she saw that the stone had been rolled away and the tomb was open, she turned and ran back to the disciples, crying, "They've stolen the Lord's body! And I have no idea where it is!"

So Peter and John took off running to the tomb to see for themselves. John outran Peter and got there first. Looking inside, he saw the linen grave sheets, but no body. But he didn't actually go in. Then Peter came and went right inside. He saw the linen grave sheets and the folded head scarf lying to one side by itself. Then John went in and he, too, saw the folded head scarf and began to believe that Jesus had risen from the dead. Until that point they didn't understand what the scripture meant when it said that He would rise from the dead. Still a little puzzled, they went back to their homes.

Mary got back to the tomb after the two disciples had gone. For a moment she stood there crying and then decided to look inside. When she did, she saw two angels in white robes, sitting one at the head and the other at the feet where Jesus' body had been. They asked, "Why are you crying?"

She answered, "Because they have stolen the Lord's body, and I don't know where it is." Then she turned, and through her tears she noticed Someone standing nearby. The Man said, "Why are you crying?" She thought it was the caretaker for the little garden and answered, "Sir, if you've taken the body away, tell me where it is so we can give it a proper burial."

Then Jesus called her gently by name, "Mary!" She looked up and gasped, "Teacher!"

Jesus said, "Don't touch Me and hold Me back, because I first have to go to My Father. But go to My brothers and tell them that I've gone to My Father and their Father, to my God and their God." So that's what Mary did (John 20:1–18).

When the rest of the women got to the tomb, they too saw the stone rolled away. They went inside to take care of the body, but it wasn't there. As they stood there perplexed, wondering what had happened, suddenly two men appeared, robed in white. The women were afraid, covered their faces, and bowed to the ground.

The two men asked, "Why are you looking for Someone who is alive as if He were dead? Jesus isn't here. He's risen! Remember what He told you up in Galilee? He said, 'The Son of Man will be delivered into the hands of sinful men and crucified, but on the third day He will rise from the dead.'"

Then they remembered, and with joy in their hearts they left the tomb and went to tell the disciples and the others the good news (Luke 24:1–9).

While on their way, Jesus met them and said, "Good morning!" The women could hardly believe it. They fell on their knees, held His feet, and worshipped Him. Jesus said, "Don't be afraid of me. Go and tell My brothers to go to Galilee, and I'll meet them there."

While the women were on their way to see the disciples, the Roman guards had rushed to the chief priests to tell them what had happened. When the chief priests heard it, they called a meeting to decide what to do. They offered the soldiers a large sum of money and said, "Say that during the night Jesus' disciples came and stole the body while you were sleeping." The soldiers hesitated, because sleeping on duty meant death. The priests noticed their concern, so they said, "Don't worry. If the governor hears about it, we'll satisfy him and keep you out of trouble." Then the guards took the money and agreed to lie about what had happened. To this day many Jews believe that the body of Jesus was stolen (Matt. 28:9-15).

Sunday Afternoon

Later that day two followers of Jesus were on their way to the little village of Emmaus, about seven miles from Jerusalem. They were talking about all the things that had happened during the weekend. Suddenly Jesus came up from behind, and they invited Him to walk with them, but they didn't recognize Him. He said, "You seem to be having a deep discussion about something. What is it?"

They stopped, and Cleopas looked at Him and said, "You must be from out of town. Everyone here knows what happened this past weekend in Jerusalem."

Jesus asked, "What happened?"

Cleopas answered, "The things that happened to Jesus, the prophet from Nazareth. He worked miracles and taught the people some wonderful things. There is no doubt that God was with Him. But our leaders turned Him over to the Romans, who crucified Him. We believed that He was the Messiah, and we were hoping that He would deliver us from the Romans. But He's been dead for three days. And this morning some of the women went to the tomb where He had been buried and found it empty. They said something about seeing angels, who told them that He was alive. Two of the disciples ran to the tomb and also found it empty, just as the women had said, but they didn't see Jesus."

Jesus responded, "Don't be foolish enough to let your faith be affected by what just happened. You need to put your faith in Scripture and what the prophets said about the Messiah. He had to suffer and die to show His glory. Come, let's walk and talk." So, beginning with Moses and on through the prophets, He explained to them those passages that talked about Himself.

As they approached the village, it looked to them as if Jesus were going on. So they urged Him to stay, saying, "It's already getting dark. It would be better for You to stay with us."

He agreed. When they sat down to eat, they asked Him to offer the blessing. He prayed, took the bread, broke it in half, and passed it to each of them. Suddenly their eyes were opened, and they recognized Him. But, just as quickly, He disappeared.

They said to each other, "Didn't our hearts feel as if they were on fire while He talked to us and explained the prophecies in Scripture? This is the Lord! He's alive!"

So they left their meal and ran back to Jerusalem, stumbling along in the dark, to tell the disciples what had happened. By the time they got there, it was late evening. They found the disciples and the others who were with them excited, saying to each other, "It's true! The Lord is alive! He appeared to Peter!"

Then Cleopas and his friend told them what had happened to them on the road, and that they recognized the Lord by the way He said the blessing and broke the bread (Luke 24:13-35).

Earlier that same day, which was Sunday, the disciples had met, but had locked the door for fear of the Jews (John 20:19).

Suddenly Jesus stood in the room and said, "Peace to all of you." They were afraid because they thought it was a spirit. He said to them, "Why are you so scared? Why do you refuse to believe? Look at My hands and feet. Can't you see that it's really Me? Come and feel Me. A spirit doesn't have flesh and bones." Then He showed them His wounded hands and feet.

While they stood there with their hearts full of joy, thinking that it was too good to be true that Jesus was right there with them, He said, "Do you have something to eat?" They gave Him a piece of broiled fish and honeycomb, and He ate them.

Afterward He said to them, "What has happened this weekend is what I was telling you would happen when I was still with you. Everything written about Me in the Scriptures, from Moses to the prophets and in the Psalms, had to be fulfilled." Then He opened their minds so that they could understand the Scriptures and said, "It was written that the Messiah would suffer, die, and rise from the grave on the third day, and that repentance and forgiveness would be preached to all nations, beginning at Jerusalem. You are my witnesses because you saw all these things happen to Me. I will send you what my Father promised. But stay in Jerusalem until you receive power from heaven to carry out your mission" (Luke 24:36-49).

Then He took a deep breath and said, "Receive the Holy Spirit. He will be your guide. If you tell someone about repentance and forgiveness and he repents, his sins will be forgiven, but if he does not repent, his sins will remain (John 20:22, 23).

The Next Sunday

The evening that Jesus appeared to the disciples, Thomas wasn't there. When he came back, they said, "Thomas! The Lord is alive! He was here! We've seen Him and talked with Him!"

Thomas replied, "Unless I see Him for myself, and see the scars in His hands and feet, and touch the wound in His side, I refuse to believe it."

A week later, when all the disciples were together again and the door was locked, suddenly Jesus stood in their midst and said, "Peace to all of you." Then He looked at Thomas and said, "Come over here and take a look at the scars on My hands and feet, and touch the wound in My side. Don't keep doubting. Believe what you see."

Thomas was stunned and for a moment stood there speechless. Then he fell on his knees and cried out, "You are the Lord, and you are my God!" Jesus said, "Thomas, you believe because you have seen Me. Blessed are those who have not seen Me and yet believe" (John 20:24-29).

twenty seven

Breakfast by the Lake

Jesus had promised His disciples that He would meet them by the Lake of Galilee. Seven of them gathered there: Peter, Thomas, Nathaniel, James and John, and two others. As they waited for Jesus, Peter stood up and said, "I'm going fishing." The others responded, "Wait a minute and we'll go with you." So late that afternoon they got into the boat and fished all night, but they caught nothing. Just as the sun was coming up and they were rowing back to shore, they saw a man standing on the beach. They didn't know it was Jesus. He called out to them, "Did you catch any fish?"

They answered, "No!"

"Throw out your net on the right side of the boat," He called back, "and you'll catch some!" They did, and soon their net was so full of fish they had a hard time pulling it in.

Then John realized the man on the beach was Jesus, and he called to Peter, "That's the Lord!" When Peter heard that, he grabbed his outer robe, quickly put it on because he was stripped for work, tucked it into his belt, jumped into the water, and headed for the beach. The others stayed in the boat, which was still about 100 yards from shore, and brought it in, dragging the net full of fish behind them.

When they got there, they saw a charcoal fire with fish cooking on it and bread to one side. Jesus said, "Bring some of the fish you caught." Peter rushed over to help them pull the nets ashore. They counted 153 big fish, and yet their net had not torn!

Jesus said, "Come, let's sit down and have breakfast." Not one of them asked who He was, because they knew it was Jesus. Then He took the bread and the fish and gave it to them. This was the third time Jesus had appeared to His disciples since the resurrection.

After breakfast Jesus asked Peter, "Peter, do you love Me more than these?"

Peter answered, "Lord, I love You—You know that."

Jesus said, "That's good. Feed my lambs."

He asked Peter again, "Do you really love Me?"

Peter responded, "Lord, You know how much I love You."

Jesus said, "Take care of My sheep." Then He asked Peter a third time, "Peter, how much do you love Me?"

Peter was hurt when Jesus asked him a third time, and said, "Lord, You know everything about me. You know that deep down I do love You."

Jesus replied, "Feed My sheep."

Then Jesus looked at Peter and said, "When you were young and strong, you put on your clothes and went wherever you wanted to go. But when you're old, you will stretch out your arms, they will strip you of your clothes, and then take you where you don't want to go." By saying this, Jesus was telling Peter the kind of death he would die, which would be to glorify God. Then He said, "Remember—follow Me."

As the disciples were walking along the beach, Peter turned and noticed John following close behind. So he asked Jesus, "Lord, what about this man—what will happen to him?"

Jesus answered, "If I want him to live until I come back, what is that to you? *You* follow Me."

Then the rumor got started that John would never die. But Jesus didn't say that—He said, "If I want him to live until I come back, what is that to you?" (John 21:1-23).

Their Final Meeting

Later the disciples went to the mountain in Galilee where Jesus had arranged to meet them. When He arrived, they worshipped Him, but some still had unanswered questions. Jesus talked with them and said, "I have been given full authority in heaven and on earth. I want you to go and make disciples of all nations, and baptize them in the name of the Father, the Son, and the Holy Spirit. Teach them everything I have taught you, and I'll be with you to the end of the world" (Matt. 28:16-20).

A Goodbye and a Promise

Near the end of the 40 days with His disciples, they were all back in Jerusalem with Jesus. He led them toward Bethany to the top of the Mount of Olives. Raising His hands, He blessed them, and as He did so, He was lifted off the ground and began ascending to heaven (Luke 24:50, 51; Acts 1:3).

As the disciples watched Him go up, a cloud soon covered Him, and He disappeared from sight. They kept looking up, hoping to catch another glimpse of Him. Suddenly two men dressed in white robes stood next to them and said, "Men of Galilee, why are you standing here staring into an empty sky? Jesus is going home, but someday this same Jesus will come back in the clouds of heaven just as you've seen Him go" (Acts 1:10, 11).

Then they returned to Jerusalem with great joy in their hearts, and were often in the Temple praising God and thanking Him for what He had done (Luke 24:52, 53).

It's True

Now, these things were written that you might believe that Jesus is the Son of God, and by believing in Him have eternal life. These things that we have written are true. There were many, many other things that Jesus did that we could have written about. If all the things about Him were known and could be written, all the libraries of the world wouldn't be big enough to hold all the books (John 20:31; 21:24, 25).

SATISFYING THE LONGING OF YOUR SOUL

Hunger reveals how you can truly encounter God and have a close relationship with Him. You'll discover the joy and fulfillment of such spiritual practices as simplicity, solitude, worship, community, and fasting. With fresh insight and practical guidance Jon L. Dybdahl leads you on a journey that will satisfy the longing of your soul. 978-0-8127-0458-7. Paperback. 144 pages.

3 WAYS TO SHOP

- Visit your local ABC
- Call 1-800-765-6955
- www.AdventistBookCenter.com

WHY DO WE NEED GOD WHEN WE SEEM TO HAVE ALL WE NEED?

Seven Reasons Why Life Is Better With God

Nathan Brown

Christianity is often styled as an answer to our problems, particularly for those who have no options left. But what about those who seem to have everything going for them? who are well off, well fed, well educated, faced with many different opportunities, and apparently doing OK?

The truth is that we don't have to hit rock bottom to need God. This book ponders seven reasons life is better with God—when things are bad, God can make them better; when things are good, God makes them better still. 978-0-8127-0436-5. Paperback, 160 pages.

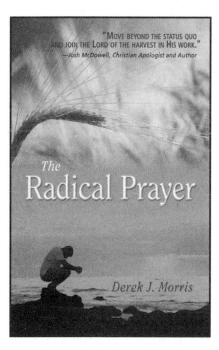

IS YOUR FAITH BUILT ON A MIRACLE-DISPENSING GOD?

RICHARD JENSEN

Miracles, Faith, and
UNANSWERED PRAYER

IS YOUR FAITH BUILT ON
A MIRACLE-DISPENSING GOD?

Miracles, Faith, and Unanswered Prayer

Why does God answer some prayers and not others? Why do some people seem to experience miracles, while others don't? Does God play favorites? Richard Jensen tackles some of life's thorny questions in this straightforward exploration of Christian faith—and what it is not. 978-0-8280-2015-2. Paperback, 231 pages.

3 WAYS TO SHOP
- Visit your local ABC
- Call 1-800-765-6955
- www.AdventistBookCenter.com

REVIEW AND HERALD®
PUBLISHING ASSOCIATION
Since 1861 · www.reviewandherald.com